THE LEGACY OF MAURICE PEKARSKY

The Legacy

of Maurice Pekarsky

Edited with an Introduction by Alfred Jospe

Foreword by A. L. Sachar

Chicago | QUADRANGLE BOOKS | 1965

FOREWORD

The preparation of this volume has been, I well know, a reverent act, a form of *Kaddish* for a beloved friend. Alfred Jospe, in his introduction, interprets with mastery the resourceful mind and the compassionate heart of Maurice Pekarsky. But as an editor of integrity, he frankly states Maurice's frustrating status as non-writer—frustrating because Maurice was genuinely articulate, exciting, and communicative. That this man should have gone virtually unrecorded, except for bits and pieces, is a further convincing argument for the development of oral history of taped dialogue for libraries. Maurice's inner convictions, so easily and informally conveyed, should have been captured in his own voice so that we might hear, and then permanently preserve, the magic of his love and his serene, wholesome faith that life is good, that Jewishness has contemporary significance and enduring potency, that the often devastating loneliness of living can be mastered. Knowing that such an opportunity has been irretrievably lost must have made Dr. Jospe's task as editor a heartbreaking one.

This is not to say that the present posthumous volume is

merely an act of memorial respect. The reconstructed compilation is valuable. It was imperative that what has survived of Maurice be brought together in one place. For those who never knew him, and who must rely upon his fragmentary literary estate for the igniting spark, I can only express regret. How much poorer they are for missing the opportunity to have Maurice listen to them! For the heart of Maurice's secret was the one gift Solomon asked of the Lord—"a listening heart." Yet we do hear it in these pages, and nowhere more clearly than in his personal, uninhibited, chatty letters from Israel where Maurice wryly draws the distinction between being "houseless" and being "homeless." His instinct for substantive precision is fortunately captured. His astonishingly effective technique in teaching, his ability to draw the best from the student in the literal meaning of "educate," leading out, are all here, at least enough to indicate the power of the man's friendship. So there is reward enough for the reader.

Let me return to "the listening heart" which made Maurice the incomparable teacher that he was. Apparently he had this gift from the outset of his career. I sensed it thirty years ago when I was responsible for the national Hillel program and recruited him for one of the earliest established Foundations. That Maurice listened to me then, and accepted the call to Cornell, proved to be a turning point for the Hillel family and its welfare. Yet I cannot take full credit even for the recruitment, for I believe that Maurice listened to his own heart as well as to my invitation.

As a Jew, Maurice was an enviable man. I write this knowing that Maurice himself would undoubtedly be startled by any such appraisal. What is an enviable Jew? Rich in worldly goods? Maurice was completely dependent upon his wife, Nell, to keep track of a budget at which beginners in professional life today often sneer. Well endowed with health? Maurice was a frail man who expended himself fiercely though always cheerfully. Learned? This he was, but to be

6

learned per se, to be master of the legacy of his ancestors for pride's sake, was not Maurice. No, what one envied in Maurice was his perfect clarity (and his charity, too) about his own Jewishness. His was no negative faith; he was serenely positive in his relationship to a living God. He stood calmly, happily, in the full spate of Jewish history. Yet he understood and had compassion for "the Canaanite" in so many of us. He had tenderness for the restive displacement of many American Jews, even while he gently deplored the sentimentality and parochialism of "social Judaism." In his Israeli incumbency he had appreciation for the turbulent, often arrogant, spirit of the sabras even while he hoped, audibly and uncompromisingly, for ways in which to instill spiritual awareness into their lives. And through all his unroutinized career, there rollicked an unquenchable sense of humor, most often self-deprecatory.

For the rest, what is there to say? All the adjectives that come to mind with Maurice's name and that the editor notes, are suffused with light: "an incandescent teacher," "a luminous thinker," "a shining personality." Maurice truly had an inner fire that warmed without burning, that glowed without searing, and the legions of his students carried brightness away with them from his presence.

Maurice's aptest references came from his Judaic background. But perhaps the meaning of such communicable brightness was best caught in Shelley's "Adonais":

> . . . The pure spirit shall flow
> Back to the burning fountain whence it came,
> A portion of the Eternal, which must glow
> Through time and change, unquenchably the
>   same . . .
>
> Truly, he has outsoared the shadow of our night.

A. L. SACHAR

Brandeis University

7

EDITOR'S NOTE

Maurice Bernard Pekarsky was born in Jedwabno, Poland, on July 10, 1905. He spent his adolescent years in Grand Rapids, Michigan, where his family had settled in 1921, attended the University of Michigan, from which he was graduated *cum laude* in 1930, and pursued graduate studies in social psychology at the University of California and at the University of Iowa under Professor Kurt Lewin.

Upon his ordination by the Jewish Institute of Religion in 1933, he joined the Hillel program and remained associated with it throughout his rabbinic career, first as director of the B'nai B'rith Hillel Foundation at Cornell University (1933-1937), then as director of the program at Northwestern University (1937-1940), and from 1940 on at the University of Chicago. He also served as director of Hillel's Department of Leadership Training and founded the National Hillel Summer Institute, which he guided from its inception in 1946 until his death. In 1950 Rabbi Pekarsky and his family went to Israel where he established the Hillel program at the Hebrew University in Jerusalem. He and his family returned to Chicago in 1955.

Rabbi Pekarsky died of a heart attack on July 11, 1962, at the age of fifty-seven.

* * *

During the last years of his life, Maurice Pekarsky had hoped to find the time for a systematic development of his thoughts and reflections on Jewish life and Jewish education. But death intervened, and the papers he left contained few complete manuscripts. They consisted mainly of brief outlines, lecture notes, and fragments—ideas and formulations he had jotted down as they occurred to him or struggled for expression.

Had he lived to publish a volume of his own, he would have polished each phrase and sentence until it reflected every nuance of what he wished to communicate. I felt, however, that it would be best to edit only lightly in order to preserve the spontaneity and immediacy of Pekarsky's speaking style to the greatest possible degree.

The section on Jewish student life and some aspects of the work of the B'nai B'rith Hillel Foundations was included because it represents Pekarsky's main personal and professional concerns throughout his career. Although the papers in this section set forth his reflections on what may seem to be a highly specialized field of Jewish education, they actually deal with issues which go far beyond the confines of the college campus. They touch questions which are fundamental to Jewish education and existence in our time.

I want to record my gratitude to Rabbi Richard Winograd for his assistance in the editorial preparation of several selections, to Professor Ralph Lerner of the University of Chicago for his careful reading of the manuscript and his valuable suggestions, to the editors of Quadrangle Books for their encouragement and cooperation, and to the Rabbinical Assembly of America for the permission to reprint, with slight changes, the paper on "Religion in Israel" from *Proceedings*

EDITOR'S NOTE

1956. The publication of this volume has been facilitated by contributions made, in Maurice Pekarsky's memory, by his colleagues and friends on the B'nai B'rith Hillel Commission, by the members of the National Association of Hillel Directors, and by numerous other individuals in all parts of the country.

ALFRED JOSPE

CONTENTS

To write of Maurice Pekarsky's legacy is more than an act of piety or love or the evocation of a great teacher and an incandescent personality. It is an attempt to focus on some of the central issues of contemporary Jewish life and to explore how Pekarsky's thoughts can clarify our understanding of the meaning and implications of Jewish identity, the relevance of the Jewish tradition for modern man and the Jewish person in our time, and the problems of Jewish education in the United States, especially among Jewish college students today.

There are several reasons why it is difficult to give a systematic account of Pekarsky's legacy. He would have been the first to object to the publication of this book. Had we been able to consult him, he would have laughed and made fun of us—and of himself—in his gentle manner which never hurt even when it was meant to deflate you; and he would have vetoed the plan even though secretly he would have been pleased by it. Masterful as he was in his ability to summarize a complex discussion, he distrusted quick summaries and final formulations. He knew that a person is so much more than the sum total of what can be said about him, and he was deeply sensitive to the fact that life defies easy generalizations, that verbal facility may produce oratorical fireworks which titillate the speaker's ego but do not touch the problem, and that quick formulations cannot capture the richness of a man's life—his aspirations as well as his accommodations, his deepest loyalties as well as the contradictions which are a part of the human condition.

Pekarsky did not leave an *opus*, a body of writings. His files were full of little scraps of paper on which he had jotted down observations or new formulations. Even when he was alone, he was engaged in a continuous dialogue with people he had met and books he had read. He was constantly making notes—on the backs of envelopes, on bills, on restaurant menus. But he did not write. His medium of self-expression was the spoken word. He was a teacher, not a writer, and he was at his best when he could be spontaneous and relate to a person. Though not a flashy orator, Pekarsky was enormously gifted as a speaker. When he spoke to you, he really addressed you: he challenged your assumptions, illumined your predicaments, compelled you to think with him, and spoke to your deepest concerns as Jew and human being or, as he liked to put it, as human-being-born-Jew. But he was no writer and did not write.

Interestingly enough, Pekarsky rarely spoke to a group extemporaneously, even though it was one of his little vanities to make us think otherwise. When I began to sift his notes and papers, I was struck by the fact that I sometimes discovered six or seven drafts of the same speech—none complete, each different from the other, each ending in the middle of a different sentence or word. Nell Pekarsky told me how hard her husband would work in preparing a lecture or speech; often, he pounded away at the typewriter for hours, crossing out, reformulating, starting all over again, until the thought he wanted to bring out was clear in his mind—and then he stopped in the middle of the sentence. He had gained the clarity he needed.

But to write a manuscript was agony for him. As patient, lenient, and understanding as he was with the fumbling efforts of others, as demanding was he of himself. He was keenly aware that the printed word is frozen into finality, and he was never satisfied that what he had said or tried to write really achieved that degree of inner coherence and clarity of thought he wanted.

Above all, it is difficult to extract a comprehensive account of Pekarsky's views from the material that is available to us because he was a man of many facets. His personality embraced a bundle of fascinating contradictions. A child of East and West, he fused both in his personality and outlook. Embedded in the tradition of religion, he understood the validity of doubt and skepticism and defended their right to be heard. A graduate of the religiously liberal Jewish Institute of Religion, he possessed the heart and spiritual proclivities of a Lubavitcher *chossid*.[1] He was a rationalist whose analytical mind was tinged with mysticism, a "realist with the soul of a poet" (as Charles Shulman put it); a profoundly and unequivocally committed Jew whose world view could offer warm hospitality to other faiths and philosophies; a man who communicated with his God through the traditional disciplines of worship, study, and *mitzvah*,[2] but also found a gate to heaven in the glorious sunset over Lake Michigan or in Beethoven's *Missa Solemnis*.

I have always been fascinated by what I felt was his similarity to another man whom the Jewish world of his time had designated as the Jewish Plato—Moses Mendelssohn. Both were products of tradition as well as of modernity. And both

---

1. Member of the HaBaD group of Hasidism founded by Rabbi Shneor Zalman of Liady in White Russia over 150 years ago. While Hasidism in general espoused the emotional and intuitive, HaBaD (which stands for *Hokhmah*—Wisdom, *Binah*—Understanding, *Da'at*—Knowledge) emphasizes the intellectual and rational elements in man's relationship to God.

2. "Commandment," religious obligation.

sought to find a way to reconcile intellectually what they were able to fuse in their personal lives: *Torah* and *hokh-mah*,[3] faith and reason, the truth that claims to originate in God's revelation and the truth that claims to originate in man's reason; the world view that proceeds from the mystery to the known and the world view that starts with the known and seeks to push its frontiers ever deeper into the mystery.

Both were trying to harmonize these two worlds intellectually. But here the similarity ends. Mendelssohn argued as a philosopher, setting forth certain propositions about the nature of God and religion which he considered self-evident to reason in consonance with the religious rationalism of his time. Pekarsky did not argue on the philosophical level, though he could do that, too. What ultimately mattered to him most was not theology, but psychology. To use Karl Jasper's terminology, what was significant to him as an educator was not objective, but subjective truth; not logical analysis or verification of certain abstract propositions, but the psychological implications of man's position—the impact which a person's faith in or rejection of God might have upon his own life, and the consequences which his affirmations or denials might have for him in his search for a sense of at-homeness in the universe.

Pekarsky's educational method did not limit itself to this shift from theology to psychology; he also substituted *charisma* for *dogma*—the power and contagion of a compelling personal persuasiveness for the statement of an officially formulated, authoritative credal position. To put it differently, he replaced the exposition of the *halakhah*[4] of Jewish tradition with the exploration of the *halikhah* of man's needs,

3. *Torah*: "teaching" or "law." In a broader sense, *Torah* also denotes the total body of traditional Jewish thought and teaching which derives its validity from the divine revelation at Sinai. *Hokhmah*: "intelligence," "wisdom," or "science." Used here to denote secular learning.

4. "Law," derived from *halakh*, to go or follow. The term denotes the legal portions of talmudic and later Jewish literature.

concerns, and predicaments in the face of the demands of tradition.

Thus, he never told you to accept something on faith or because tradition demanded it of you. He was quick to sense the intellectual or emotional difficulties you might have with the presuppositions or some particular view of Jewish tradition, and he would gently begin probing your assumptions and question your own questioning until he had enlarged your understanding of what this particular concept might have meant in its original context and what it might contribute to your understanding of man's condition today. As one of his friends at the University of Chicago put it, he was the only rabbi he had ever known who "could lead without oppressing and whose wit and intelligence were such that his intellectual and moral position was made eminently compelling and meaningful to his friends and students alike."

This was the reason for his singular effectiveness in personal and group conversations, but also for our occasional exasperation with him. When you asked him a question you rarely got an answer. What you got was a reformulation of your question so as to show you the kind of question you should have asked. Or he gave you an analysis of the problems and issues which your question raised, and of the various alternatives you had of looking at the entire problem area. But you took it from Pekarsky because you sensed his concern behind the method. And even though we knew—and he knew that we knew—that he employed this method often simply to gain time to clarify his own thinking, we went along with him because we also knew that he wanted to make us think. Instead of handing out an answer which might emerge from his experience but would not necessarily address itself to our particular situation, he tried to help us make something out of our own thrust into the mystery of things.

I

What then is Maurice Pekarsky's legacy?

First, he gave all who worked with him a heightened awareness of the importance of the dialectical method in the educational process. Let me put it more subtly. In all his human relationships, Pekarsky was a dialogical person *par excellence*. In an educational situation, however, he employed the dialectical method. He was convinced that Socrates had been right when he insisted that teaching is the art of elucidation by elicitation, and that the true teacher does not impose his mind upon his students but tries to get the students to use theirs. Therefore, he loved to "pull a Pekarsky" on people— to encourage a dialogue in which he himself would merely ask casual questions in order to stimulate others to talk, to formulate their ideas and views, to clear up misconceptions, and thus to achieve clarity.

The method usually was very effective except when he encountered people who had mastered the same approach. This happened, for instance, in a discussion with Martin Buber shortly after Pekarsky's arrival in Israel. His report about the meeting reveals as much about Pekarsky as it does about Buber:

> I found my usual technique of questioning my interlocutor failing me as the master of the *I and Thou* insisted gently but persistently on turning the tables on me. Until I met him, I managed to have people tell me what they thought Hillel should do at the Hebrew University and what students required. But the gentle and wise Buber wanted to know what *I* had come for. I kept telling him that the program of the Foundation was

to emerge from the needs and interests of the students here, and that my task in these early days was to discover the nature of the university, the students, and the community. But all to no avail. He admitted that this was a wise and necessary procedure but kept pushing me to tell him what my ultimate objective was. He broke down my resistance. I admitted the failure of my position as the leader in the dialogue and proceeded to unfold for him my conception of the purpose and function of Hillel at the Hebrew University."

Some simple but, I think, compelling conclusions emerge from his insistence on method. One is touchingly intimated in a letter which a student at Purdue University wrote to Nell Pekarsky after her husband's death: "Whenever I feel that I am getting nowhere in my education, I always think of his words which were his trademark: 'We came here not to answer questions but to raise them.' But the questions he raised have answered an awful lot of my questions."

A second conclusion: the mark of the true educator is his ability to listen. Pekarsky, who had been a co-worker and close friend of Kurt Lewin (1890-1947), the well-known psychologist and Director of the Research Center for Social Dynamics at the Massachusetts Institute of Technology, delivered the eulogy at Lewin's funeral in Cambridge in 1947. What he said about Kurt Lewin at that time is probably the best description of Pekarsky's own motivation and aspirations:

> The essence of Kurt Lewin's wisdom lay in his profoundly human qualities of sympathy and love for persons, for the suffering and the alienated. He listened to everyone and learned from everyone— a chance conversation in a restaurant, the notions

> of a student, the criticisms of the learned. He lis-
> tened to all. . . . He was as eager to learn as to
> teach—eager to learn so that he might teach.

This is how I believe Pekarsky also envisioned his own life and role. All kinds of people came to him for conversation or counsel—students and faculty members, close friends and chance acquaintances, Jews and Christians, young and old, a *chossid* from Canada, a young Negro writer, a Presbyterian minister, a Catholic father, a fraternity house cook who liked to think about him when she felt tired or just wanted to be encouraged by the warmth of his smile. No one was ever turned away. He listened carefully to all. His technique of establishing rapport with people can be described, but no description can capture the magic of the personality behind the technique. What communicated itself instantly to every-one was the feeling that this man was genuinely interested in you, that he had an understanding of man's frailties as well as his strengths, and that he did not simply counsel "profes-sionally" but could be a trusted friend.

He had an uncanny ability to ask questions that would penetrate beyond the often fumbling or self-protective verbal expression of a problem and go right to the heart of the real questions that troubled the person facing him. When he felt he understood a problem he was willing to comment. He commented honestly and did not hesitate to encourage by criticism, to make a value judgment, to offer advice or sug-gest some specific course of action at a time when profes-sional counselors were frequently bending over backwards to be neutral and non-directive.

Pekarsky "listened" in other ways. When he saw some-one troubled or depressed he would go out of his way to encourage him to speak. A student once told Nell Pekarsky that her husband had saved his life when, early one morning, he stopped at the booth in the campus drugstore where the young man was sitting, staring into space, a picture of despair. Pekarsky asked him with a smile, "What do you know?"—one of his pet phrases with which he liked to initiate a conversation. "I had the feeling this man really wanted to know," said the student, "and out poured my heart."

Pekarsky urged us to train ourselves, indeed to discipline ourselves, to listen, even where we think we have an answer or know better. For to listen means that our response to the questions of others is determined by the nature of their problems and not by our own needs and concerns.

II

I have already mentioned Pekarsky's concern for people. It is a second facet of his legacy.

His emphasis on method was more than a preference for an effective educational device. It was the expression of his profound respect and concern for persons as persons—a concern that was central to his whole being. This was not a professional stance, the skillful demonstration of rabbinical bedside manners. No matter how busy, preoccupied, or tired he was, he always had time for others. And he had the ability to make everyone feel that he was his personal friend— as indeed he was. He encouraged them to speak. He wanted to know what was on a man's mind and in his heart. Therefore, in the words he had applied to Lewin, he was able to cross the barriers of geography and language into the hearts and minds of countless men and women with whom he developed a personal relationship.

Here is the key term: personal relations. This was a vital personal need. But it was just as much a central concept in his philosophy of education. Education, for him, was a genuine dialogue between teacher and student. In the growing institutionalization of our society, which affects educational and religious enterprises as much as it does other groupings, the personal bond between teacher and student was for Pekarsky the significant factor in the education of young people. In fact, he said more than once that his happiest years in Hillel had been those early years at Cornell, Northwestern, Chicago, and at the Hebrew University, when he did not yet have to worry about a building. In his scheme of things, houselessness was not homelessness. The physical structure was replaced by the relationship between student and Hillel director. Hillel was where he was. He always had students at his home; its doors were always wide open; it became the base of his activity. He arranged to meet students in the student union, the corner drugstore—or its Jerusalem equivalent, the Café Hermon on Keren Kayemet Street—where he would sit like Bernard Baruch on his park bench, transacting his business, chatting with students, asking questions, and drinking countless cups of tea.

Yet out of these meetings developed personal contacts, mutual confidences, and often lasting ties of friendship. They were ends in themselves, precious ends, but they also helped him to orient himself and to understand the students. Thus he was gradually able to develop activities which embodied the needs and concerns of the students as they became clarified in the informal give and take of these conversations.

Pekarsky reminds us that we must be concerned with students as persons. For what every young person ultimately seeks is self-discovery. What he wants is to understand what the world is, what it means to be a human being, what the options are that lie before him, and how he is to get on with others.

Formal education can deal with these questions only to a limited degree. It does not always guard itself sufficiently against the danger of succumbing to what could be called the "idolatry of verbalization," the reduction of the educational process to the transmission of data. Lectures, classes, seminars, study groups are indispensable for the communication of knowledge but address themselves mainly to a person's mind, not to his whole personality. Absorption of knowledge *per se* does not automatically cultivate the feelings, attitudes, and values which are essential to human growth. It is true, as Alfred North Whitehead said, that you cannot be wise without some basis of knowledge; but it is equally true that you may easily acquire knowledge yet remain bare of wisdom. To communicate more than facts, to impart wisdom and to deepen a person's insight and understanding of life, requires the presence of someone who can serve as a model. It requires the dialogue of hearts and minds that can emerge from a personal relationship. And Pekarsky showed us what can be done by an educator who cares for his students as individuals; who approaches them as individuals and not simply as prospective members of an organization or participants in activities; who does not wait for them to come to see him; whom they get to know not only in the classroom, in meetings, or sitting behind his desk in his office, but who seeks them out where they are, opens his home to them in warmth and friendship, and creates an atmosphere in which they can begin to sense that they are his most important concern.

III

Pekarsky's concern for people is also the key to a third facet of his legacy—his approach to the problems of Jewish persons in our time. I have already indicated that he was deeply preoccupied with what probably is the fundamental issue which has confronted the Jew since the Emancipation: the tension between tradition and modernity, the question of how to live as a Jew in the modern world without surrendering either the claims of Judaism to the values of the world or the claims of the world to the values of Judaism.

Pekarsky saw clearly that this is the fundamental problem of the modern Jew. But once again he preferred to examine the issues in psychological rather than in purely theological terms. Like Kurt Lewin, he attempted to understand the modern Jew psychologically. For Pekarsky, the story of the Jews since the French Revolution has been essentially the history of a whole people in search of a definition. It is the story of the violent disintegration of the historic image Jews had of themselves, and of their attempts to recast the shattered fragments, the broken tablets of the Law, into a meaningful explanation of their experience, existence, and destiny in the world.

This is the ultimate religious and psychological problem of Jews in our time. They are in search of an orientation and understanding that will give them a sense of at-homeness in the world they inhabit, a clear and satisfying image of themselves, a feeling that their life as Jews makes sense and has meaning.

From this starting point, Pekarsky went on to define the problem more deeply. He pointed out that the Jews in the ghetto did not have this predicament, because they had an image of themselves that gave meaning and direction to their lives.

In Pekarsky's analysis of this historic image we encounter one of his particularly telling concepts. It was not original with him, but he employed it in an original way. The image a person has of himself is embodied in particular ways of acting, thinking, and feeling. Thought, act, and emotion—this triple relationship embodies the way we all relate to something meaningful. The thought must explain the act adequately; the act must embody and express the thought adequately; and we must feel satisfied that what we think and do is good and right and worthwhile.

Pekarsky felt that Jews were related to their tradition in

these three ways. On the level of *thought*, they had a conception of the universe which affirmed God as the source of all life, power, and meaning. He had elected Israel to be an *am kadosh*, a holy people. He would punish and exile His people when they strayed from His path but would ultimately vindicate them, and His final act of redemption would justify the suffering that had preceded it.

On the level of *act*, the Jewish religion was not so much a theological system as a solid psychological matrix surrounding an individual's life from birth to death, enclosing all the ordinary and extraordinary occasions in sacrament and ritual. Finally, on the level of *sentiment*, there was the feeling that it was good and meaningful to be a Jew.

The predicament of the modern Jew, according to Pekarsky, is that the wholeness and unity of this relationship were shattered by the movement of the Jew into the modern world. It was a movement from a setting in which Judaism was a majority culture—and in the ghetto it was a majority culture—to a Judaism that became a minority culture in its new setting of actual or presumed freedom. It was a movement from what Leo Baeck once called *Milieufroemmigkeit* to *Individualfroemmigkeit*—from a setting in which the Jew lived in a total Jewish milieu and in which Judaism was the matrix and context of his individual experiences, to a setting in which the non-Jewish world is the dominant milieu, in which Judaism is no longer the context of the individual's whole experience and expression, and in which he must make a conscious and deliberate personal effort to define and justify the nature of the difference between himself and the majority. It was a movement from a world in which the experiences of the Jew were sufficient to explain and validate his existence as a Jew, to a world in which he needs a verbal definition of his identity because he lacks the definition which comes from his experience of Jewishness. In the past there had been an organic unity of thought, act, and emotion; now, for many Jews, the thought is no longer adequate to explain the act, the act is no longer suitable to embody the thought, and the sentiment is ambivalent. Above all, it was a movement from a world limited in space but unlimited in time, to a world in which the Jew has acquired the world of space but has largely lost his sense of time in the process.

Yet, as Pekarsky pointed out time and again, we cannot define a Jew except in terms of some historic context, that is, in a time dimension. When he spoke of time dimension, he did not, of course, refer to a detached academic investigation; time dimension means the experience of the past as contemporary event.

The ghetto possessed this time dimension. Life in the ghetto was actually defined by two conditions. Spatially, the *shtetl* was separated from its neighbors: it had a boundary line that kept Jews apart from non-Jews. But in addition to the boundary line there also was what Pekarsky liked to call a "gatekeeper" who enforced the separation. Where there is a boundary line but no gatekeeper, you have freedom of mobility; you can move whenever you want to. The *shtetl*, however, had a boundary line as well as a gatekeeper—the pressure of the non-Jewish majority, a governmental edict, municipal laws, other restrictive factors which prevented the Jews from moving from one area to another, that is, into the non-Jewish world.

Yet although the Jews of the ghetto could not move in space, they were able to move in time. Pekarsky was fond of quoting the opening lines of *Life Is With People:* "The shtetl traces its descent from creation and Sinai." Before the Emancipation, the Jew was able to travel in time. His entire way of life was so structured that everything he did related him to time—it related him to Sinai, to creation, to Abraham, Moses, Hillel, and Akiba.

Thus, "Jewish time," in Pekarsky's definition, is the experience of the past as contemporary event. "You begin to sense your own link with Abraham, Isaac, and Jacob, with Moses, Jeremiah, and Spinoza, with pious Jews and heretics, with good Jews and bad Jews, with lowly Jews and wealthy Jews, with saints and sinners, with all kinds of Jews." They all are part of our time dimension; and only "when you begin to sense your relationship with them is there some possibility of meaning for Jewish life and Jewish experience in our time."

IV

Pekarsky used these notions to explore and illumine a number of problems. He used them, for instance, to analyze the predicaments of young Jews whom he met during nearly three decades of Hillel service and especially in the 1930's and 1940's, to show their frustrations and the inner dislocations they experienced because of their attempts to sever their relationship with the Jewish past in order to overcome the stigma they thought was attached to their Jewishness and to appease or bypass the gatekeeper and gain access to the gentile world.

These notions also affected his relationship with Zionism and Israel, especially when his early Zionist ideology was put to the test of experience during his five years in Jerusalem. He discovered, with that profound anguish that exists only where one loves deeply, that Israel too has so far been able to cope with the Jewish problem primarily in terms of space and has yet to come to grips adequately and resolutely with the time dimension—the meaning and relevance of tradition. He recognized that national freedom is not an end but at most a beginning. It does not automatically solve the problem of Jewish self-definition; it merely changes its context.

Pekarsky's concept of time is, above all, however, the keystone in his philosophy of Jewish education and another facet in his legacy. What he has to say about Jewish education emerges logically from his concept of Jewish time: "If the Jewish community today wants to rediscover some sort of purpose; if it wants to begin to sense that it is not merely a speck in the sands of time but has a beginning, roots, and a future, we shall have to discover once again the means of locomotion in time." In other words, the function of Jewish education must be to provide us with the means of extending and deepening our sense of relatedness with other Jews in time. It must help us experience our descent from Sinai as contemporary event.

Pekarsky felt that American secular education fulfills this function for American children. When they study Lincoln, Jefferson, or the Civil War, when they delve into American literature or folklore, they have a means of locomotion in time. As they think about these men, read a book, or see a flag, they are reminded of something which happened in the past and sense a relationship to it. It becomes part of their life.

American Jewish education has failed to do the same for Jewish children, not only because it is often flimsy and shallow, but also because we do not give it enough time to discover "time." Above all, Jewish education in the United States has been concerned primarily with survival as a sort of therapy. Time and again Pekarsky said to his audiences: You send your youngsters to a Jewish school because you think it is good for their adjustment. Jewish education is preventive therapy so that they will know who they are if they encounter prejudice. Moreover, many of us favor Jewish education because it will make for group survival. We feel we should make Jewishness pleasant for our children so that they will remember that it is pleasant to be a Jew, avoid intermarriage, and thus enable the Jewish group to survive. But how many people ask: Survive for what?

Jewish education must of course be concerned with the problems and predicaments of Jews as Jews. It must concern itself with the particular social dislocations and psychological difficulties arising from minority status. But this is not enough. Granted that Jewish education must be so designed as to assure the survival of the Jewish group. But is this the only survival that matters? What about human survival? "Jews are human beings, too. They suffer not only as Jews. They fall in love not only as Jews. They die not only as Jews. In this world there are not only Jewish problems. There are human problems. There are those predicaments of life and death which are common to all men. A human-being-born-Jew needs more than pleasant associations with his identity." He must also be able to face intelligently and courageously the perennial questions which have disturbed the minds and hearts of all men: the great questions about life and death and suffering and evil and right and wrong and love and sex, and all the other problems that human beings must face. What does Judaism have to say to these questions? To what degree is it prepared to answer the questions of man as man? These are the issues to which Jewish education must address itself and to which it must find an answer.

And, as Pekarsky felt, it can find an answer only by recapturing the dimension of time. Thus, "the function of Jewish education today is to discover once again the means of locomotion in time, to learn to give voice to the great men and ideas of the past, and to transmute our tenuous knowledge of them into an abiding and personally experienced relationship."

This is where he ended his analysis. I often wish he hadn't, for I think that, in a deeper sense, the predicament of the modern Jew begins precisely where Pekarsky left off. We frequently discussed this point; I know he wrestled with it. One can agree with Pekarsky's statement that everything Jews did, thought, and were in the past was related to the belief in a God who was the master of the world and of man's destiny. We also know what Pekarsky meant when he said that we shall not regain that wholeness which is the essence of Jewish existence unless we recover our ability to experience our descent from Sinai as contemporary event.

But is this not precisely the question? Can we recapture this faith today? Is religious faith at all possible for modern man, and if it is, can Judaism be this faith? These questions involve a host of additional questions. Can the modern Jew who does not or cannot accept the premises of Orthodoxy still experience Sinai as contemporary event? In fact, can Sinai be a literal contemporary experience even for the modern orthodox Jew? Can the God of the *shtetl* still be the God of Times Square, Birmingham, Auschwitz, and the University of Chicago? Can Abraham, Hillel, Akiba, and all others like or unlike them still speak to us as Pekarsky envisioned? And if they do speak to us, what do they say to us that is relevant to *our* condition, that can illumine our predicaments and compete with what other world views and traditions say to us? And if we were to answer, as we are often tempted to do, that by listening to the great men in our people's past we begin at least to sense the nature and meaning of their religious experience, the question still remains: How do you recapitulate in your own life somebody else's religious experience? To paraphrase Martin Buber, speaking of God, especially of someone else's God, is not yet, and may never be, speaking to Him or hearing Him speak.

I wish Maurice Pekarsky had been granted the time to examine this problem further. In principle, however, he was right. Jewish education, in order to be Jewish education, must transcend the concerns of Jews in space and seek to recover the time dimension of Jewish life. It must create the experience of relationships which extend beyond this place and beyond this time, to the historic experiences and creative expressions which we call Jewish tradition and which alone can give Jewish persons a new wholeness of thought, act, and emotion.

Above all, Jewish education must be relevant. Horace Kallen said once (a quote which I have from Pekarsky): "I know that the heart commits itself only when it has something alive and intrepid to commit itself to, and that dead knowledge wins no living faith." Pekarsky knew that dead knowledge could win no living faith, and he taught his colleagues in pulpit and classroom that the desperate question confronting all Jewish educators is whether they do what they do in such a way that it remains dead knowledge, or whether they can make Judaism something alive and intrepid, something to which the heart can commit itself, a faith that is relevant for the modern Jew because it addresses itself to his deepest needs and ultimate concerns not only as a Jew but as a human-being-born-Jew.

V

What I have already said indicates what Pekarsky conceived to be the central role and educational task of the Hillel Foundation. He was associated with this Jewish religious and educational agency for college students from 1933 on. Upon his graduation from the Jewish Institute of Religion, he became the director of the B'nai B'rith Hillel Foundation at Cornell University; at his death in 1962, he was directing the Hillel program at the University of Chicago and simultaneously guiding Hillel's national Department of Leadership Training.

Throughout these years he was repeatedly offered promotions or invited to move from the college campus to posts of national significance in other fields of Jewish education or communal service. He could have served as National Hillel Director. He was invited to accept a position with the Hebrew University, to head a college of Jewish studies in the United States, to direct the program of an international agency for Jewish education. Pekarsky turned down all offers. He wanted to remain where he was, on the campus. He knew his place was not among the administrators and technicians of education but among the students. The university was his intellectual locale, and his calling was to stimulate and guide young people in their quest for a faith that would give coherence, unity, and a sense of purpose and direction to their lives.

He was especially concerned with the questions and predicaments which he felt troubled many young Jews on the college campus. Between the two wars, the primary task facing Pekarsky and his colleagues in the Hillel Foundations had been to deal with the pathological features of Jewish life— to try to stem the flight of young Jews from their Jewish identity which they found intellectually irrelevant, a stigma socially, and a handicap to their career. Most students today, as Pekarsky realized, are no longer reluctant to affirm their Jewishness. But in most instances they are ignorant of what they affirm. "What they know of Jewish religion is the one-dimensional, organization-minded, and earth-bound Jewish religious culture of today. . . .Their Sunday and Hebrew School training, as they recall it, seems to have consisted largely of a series of ritual words and phrases, in Hebrew or English, a few ethical maxims and slogans, the early Biblical tales and the latest Israeli folk songs." There is little in these fragments of knowledge to call them back to their great tradition. Hence our central problem today "is no longer that Jewish students try to escape from Judaism. The problem is that Judaism is escaping them. Some of our most sensitive and thoughtful students feel that Judaism does not address itself to their concerns and predicaments as human beings in our time. It does not engage their minds even when it superficially engages their hearts. . . . It is too far removed in faith and form from what they dimly feel religion should offer."

Thus the problem of Judaism in the university community

cannot be resolved by bringing the conventional Jewish religious "denominations" to the campus, whether orthodox, conservative, or reform. It is primarily an intellectual and spiritual problem which transcends denominational and institutional identities. It does not exist solely in the university, the so-called "intellectual" community, but "the problems arising from the encounter of religion and modern culture, including contemporary Jewish culture, tend to get their sharpest definition in the university setting. Here, in the creative centers of our society and in the sensitive and responsive hearts of thoughtful and serious young men and women, Jewish religion and the synagogue are challenged as hardly anywhere else in the country."

Pekarsky felt, however, that the Jewish community should be concerned not only with its college students but also with the thousands of Jewish faculty members on American campuses. He knew that many Jewish professors have little or no contact with Jewish life. This was Pekarsky's great ache —the knowledge that the Jewish intellectual has become alienated from Jewish life, that he usually does not participate in the activities of the organized community, that he feels homeless in the Jewish community as it is today. Some intellectuals may be escapists; many are not. They usually reject the negativism and rationalizations of those who, in their public statements concerning Judaism's irrelevance to man's condition today, tend to reveal more about themselves than about Judaism. They want to be part of the Jewish community and would like to belong to its institutions for their own sake and for the sake of their children's Jewish education. Yet they are frequently repelled by the superficiality, the intellectual shallowness and babbitry that dominate much of organized Jewish life. They reject the synagogue as a social club, its frequent mediocrity and its preoccupation with campaigns rather than content. They are reluctant to accept the frequent substitution of social and entertainment values for spiritual quest. This feeling of homelessness in the organized community is probably one of the most important reasons why, in their world of ideas and intellectual concerns, Judaism is at best peripheral if it is discernible at all.

To help reclaim the Jewish intellectual for the Jewish community was thus, for Pekarsky, the central task of the Hillel Foundation. The Jewish intellectual is located in the very place in which Hillel is located, the American university. The Hillel Foundations are, or at least are supposed to be, the representatives of the Jewish intellectual tradition in the academic community. They stand "in the center of the stage on which the drama of the Jewish encounter with the Christian world and the intellectual trends of our time is taking place." Their task must be to make Jewish "time," Jewish knowledge, and Jewish faith relevant to the concerns of human beings in today's world.

Hillel's ability to meet this challenge, however, requires people who are equipped for it. Here emerges Pekarsky's concept of the Hillel director and, indeed, of the modern rabbi. He frequently analyzed the functions and predicaments of the Hillel director and liked to define him as "the lonely man" on campus, as "anonymous" or "marginal" because, in the last analysis, he does not belong fully to the campus or to the Jewish community or to the community at large. Yet Pekarsky himself was the best and most convincing proof that his descriptions missed the mark. He was never lonely. He certainly was not anonymous. And instead of being marginal he stood in the very center of a vibrant Jewish life and of a community of the spirit that knew no geographic boundaries.

His definition of the role of the Hillel director was based on one central conviction. If the Jewish educator on campus is to engage students and faculty members in an intellectual dialogue within that universe of knowledge which is the university, he must be properly equipped for his task. He must be able to speak the language of the university—and by this Pekarsky did not mean the jargon of the pseudo-intellectual or the intellectual *nouveau riche*. He must study. He must read. He must eschew the comfort of routine for the discomfort of thought. He must be proficient in those areas which ultimately matter in the battle for the minds of men. This is the only possible way to close the gap between the triviality and superficiality of what we may define as "pediatric Judaism" and a Jewish identity that is as relevant intellectually as it is morally significant and emotionally satisfying.

When Pekarsky discussed these issues he usually spoke to Hillel directors; but, in the last analysis, he addressed himself to every American rabbi. In challenging his colleagues in the Hillel Foundations he ultimately challenged Jewish educators everywhere, for he knew that what is at stake today is not the American Jewish community alone but Judaism in our time and our ability to find a compelling answer to the question whether Judaism still has something to say to the world and to Jews—not something parochial or therapeutic that will relieve them of a feeling of inferiority or insecurity, but "something that will give them a sense of purpose and role both as Jews and human beings."

VI

These then are some aspects of Maurice Pekarsky's legacy. The range of his influence was enormous. Under his leadership, the Hillel Foundation at the University of Chicago became a unique intellectual and cultural center for the entire campus community, a forum for the study and discussion of vital issues of moral and social significance. He succeeded in teaching generations of college students, Jews and non-Jews alike, that religious commitment and intellectual integrity can be compatible. He was a decisive influence in the development of generations of Jewish communal workers whom he taught during his years of service as educational consultant to the Training Bureau of Jewish Communal Service. He attracted some of the great minds on the faculty of the University of Chicago to the Hillel Foundation, not only as lecturers but as members of a faculty group which continues to meet for the discussion of issues of vital concern. He succeeeded in building *Beit Hillel,* the Hillel Foundation at the Hebrew University in Jerusalem, despite the virtually insurmountable difficulties he faced as an American and a rabbi.

Much more could and perhaps should be mentioned. But the reader will be able to acquaint himself with at least that part of Pekarsky's legacy which can be recorded on the printed page. His real legacy will, however, not be found in his words we were able to recapture but in the way he affected the lives of all who knew him. Whatever our concept of immortality, Maurice Pekarsky gained that kind of immortality to which all of us aspire but which is granted only to the very few—to enter into the lives of others and to change them.

On

Part 1

Being Jewish Today

O*n Being Jewish Today* is a subject which my grandfather would not have been able to understand. To him, being Jewish was being human. Insofar as he was a well-adjusted person, he lived his Jewishness unconsciously or unselfconsciously. This abstraction, the objectification of Jewishness apart from himself, would have been inconceivable to him. Yet this is precisely the condition of the Jew in the world today. The problem of the modern Jew is that he abstracts his Jewishness from himself.

Some time ago, the father of a student at the University of Chicago came to see me about his son. The boy had been brought up in what is called a "good Jewish home." Yet the father had begun to sense his incipient estrangement. He had discovered that the boy had been "shopping around," visiting various Protestant churches, seemingly in search of self-discovery, and he asked me whether I would talk with the boy and attempt to help him think through his problems.

I looked at the student's religious preference card and found a check mark for "Jewish." Yet behind it, there was a big question mark.

I should like to suggest that this is how most of us check

"Jewishness," on a university form or elsewhere. Whether or not we put a question mark on the card, the question mark *is* there. Although we identify ourselves as Jews, we often do not know quite what this designation means. This uncertainty of definition is the ultimate religious and psychological problem of Jews in our time. They are searching for an orientation and understanding which will make it possible for them to accept the term "Jew" as a guiding principle in their relationship to themselves, to the world, and to God.

This search can be found even in the State of Israel. At the height of the recent crisis in the Middle East, the K'nesset was raising the question "What is a Jew?" The world was at the brink of war, yet Israel's leaders felt it was important to clarify the age-old issue of self-definition. In Israel the problem was a political issue. But the issue transcends politics. It is fundamental to Jewish experience in our time. The student at the University of Chicago and, in a real sense, all of us are confronted by the problem of what the word "Jew" means and represents.

This search, as I have already indicated, was not my grandfather's search. Only in the modern period do we find the disintegration of the historic image which Jews had of themselves throughout the centuries and which my grandfather embodied in his own life. The story of the Jews in the modern period is essentially the story of the violent disintegration of their historic image of themselves. At the same time, however, it is also the story of their effort to recast the shattered fragments of the image into a meaningful explanation of their experience and fate in the world.

I

The historic image Jews had of themselves was embodied in a specific conception of the cosmic drama. God is the creator of the universe, the source of all life, power, and meaning. He revealed Himself at a particular time and place in this cosmic drama—Sinai—and His revelation is contained in a particular document—the Torah—which reveals not only God's will but also the instrument He had chosen to make His will known to the world. The supreme instrument He chose is a people known as *Israel*. It is to be the *am kadosh*, a "holy people." "Ye shall be unto me a kingdom of priests and a holy nation," as the Bible says.[1]

This conception of God, Torah and Israel is embodied in specific ways of acting, thinking, and feeling. Thus, being Jewish expresses itself in the triple relationship of act, thought, and sentiment. I would add that these three elements are involved in our relationship to anything that means something to us. Even our membership in the Hillel Foundation is embodied in an act, a thought, and a sentiment. When it is embodied adequately—when there is a correspondence between act, thought, and sentiment, when the thought explains the act adequately and the act expresses the thought adequately, and when there is a feeling of satisfaction in act and thought—then we are what I call centrally related to the Hillel Foundation. When there is an inadequate, "unsatisfying" explanation of the act, when the thought does not satisfy us, when the act does not fully embody the thought, or when the sentiment is not compelling, then we are peripherally related.

1. Exodus 19:6.

Jews were bound to Jewish tradition in this triple relationship. They understood and defined their experiences in terms of this relationship. *Galut* (the destruction of their land and their dispersion through the world) was conceived as divine punishment for their sins. In the words of the prayerbook, "because of our sins we were exiled from our land." Suffering and punishment were interpreted as part of a divine plan. Everything was explained by the central idea which governed their lives. God was the master of the world, assigning destinies to individuals and to nations and choosing Israel from among the nations. Because He chose them, He expected them to live up to His will; when they sinned they were exiled.

But suffering carries with it the promise of redemption. In due time *galut* will be followed by *geulah* [redemption]. Suffering will bring redemption. Only insofar as you hold on to the traditions you brought with you to foreign lands, only insofar as you can sing the songs of Zion in a strange land, will you be able to achieve redemption. Thus, the Jews waited for the Messiah to come. The final act of redemption would justify the suffering that preceded it.

II

With the dawn of the modern age, however, Jews suddenly discovered that the image they had of themselves as the chosen among the peoples of the world was not compatible with the new knowledge which was beginning to permeate the West. Modern science and philosophy began to undermine, among Jews as well as non-Jews, the orthodox conceptions of God and the cosmic drama. Jews found it difficult to believe that they were the "chosen people" or that the Torah revealed God's plan. Indeed, many found it difficult to believe in God at all.

As a consequence, the unity of the classic triple relationship between thought, act, and emotion dissolved. The act remained in many ways, but the thought could no longer adequately justify the act. Moreover, the scientific revolution which shattered the religious image the Jew had of himself was associated with a political revolution. This speeded his civic emancipation and eliminated the factors which had compelled Jews to remain in the ghetto and maintain their separate identity.

From the viewpoint of the non-Jew, Jews have lived an underprivileged life for centuries. But what non-Jews considered underprivileged was, to the Jews, the greatest privilege—to serve as the witness and instrument of the God who had chosen them. However, they lost this sense of role and privilege when, under the impact of modernity, the image they had of themselves disintegrated. And, as they began to move out of the ghetto into the outside world, they also began to surrender the values of the ghetto to the values of the world, since it is the tendency of the underprivileged to move toward the privileged unless the underprivileged position can be vested with a cosmic or social significance.

Traditionally, Jews had thought of themselves as having a redemptive function in the cosmic and historic process. When they lost this concept, they also lost the conviction of their privileged position in relation to God. There was no God to assign this privilege to them. Therefore, they began to move out of the ghetto into the world of the gentiles. And whenever you move, whenever you travel, it is best to travel light. You drop your baggage.

This is what Jews have been doing during the past 150 years. In moving from the world of the Jews into the world of the gentiles, they have been dropping baggage—Bar Mitzvah, the Sabbath, observances, thoughts, sentiments.

I saw this migration from the ghetto to modernity in the experiences of young Jewish people at Cornell University where I began my Hillel career. Ithaca, where Cornell University is located, is very hilly. The local synagogue is in the valley while the university is on a hill. As I was leaving the synagogue on Kol Nidre night, I met a freshman who had told me earlier that he came from a strictly observant home. We walked up the hill together, and I said, "David, fasting may be difficult tomorrow. I think it is going to be hot, and when it is hot, it is hard to fast."

He said, "I suppose you are right, Rabbi, but I don't think it is going to bother me."

I commented, "I suppose you are used to it."

"Well, I am used to it, but I am not going to do it tomorrow."

"You are not going to fast tomorrow, David? I thought you were observant?"

He replied, "Yes, I have fasted ever since my Bar Mitzvah, but I won't do it tomorrow, Rabbi."

The hills of Ithaca are very steep. As we leave our father's home and move into the world, the going is also steep. The hill is the modern world with its power and attractions, its notions of success and achievement, its concepts of science, philosophy, and religion. As we go up the hill, traveling becomes difficult. Therefore we drop baggage all along the road. At times we drop an act, at times we drop a thought, and slowly the sentiment is weakened.

We are still Jewish. We go to synagogue on Yom Kippur, but we don't fast. We engage in an act, but it is unsupported by persuasive thought. The act is done without the fullness of emotional attachment. We are not performing the act because we believe in it or want to do it. We continue the act, but it no longer makes much sense.

I remember a student who asked me whether our Hillel Foundation was going to serve Passover meals. I answered that appropriate arrangements for Passover meals would be made and that the additional cost would probably be very slight—no more than five dollars for the entire week. He answered, "Well, I'll have to think about it."

He may have thought about it, but he never came back. Because of five dollars, the three-thousand-year tradition of Israel lost out. He did not eat Passover food. It was not worth five additional dollars, because it no longer made sense. He had already become a Jew who was not "centrally related"; the correspondence between act, thought, and sentiment was either artificial or inadequate. The thought no longer imbued the act with meaning, and the sentiment was ambivalent. This is the problem of being Jewish today.

We are related to the fact of our Jewishness in a fragmentary way. At times we have an act which we hold onto, but we do not quite understand the meaning of the act. At times we have a thought. We say that being Jewish implies this concept or that idea. But they are not embodied in an act. The organic relationship between act, thought, and sentiment which characterized historic Judaism is no longer available to us.

III

Certain movements in Judaism which have emerged since the Emancipation aim to solve the problem of the disintegration of the historic image.

In 1807 Napoleon called an "Assembly of Notables" to determine whether Jews could be good citizens now that they had emerged from the ghetto and were being granted civil and political rights. In the preamble to its reply, this Assembly of Notables stated that the tradition of our fathers embodies eternal verities, those religious truths handed down to us by our fathers. Because they are religious truths, they are eternal. At the same time, however, our tradition also has a national aspect: it refers to the particular experience of a particular people at particular times. Therefore the validity of this national aspect is limited to particular times and particular places. It has no claim upon us.

For the first time in our history a body of Jews divided Judaism into two components: *am*, people, and *kadosh*, holy. They made a distinction between "religion" as something universal and eternal, and "people" as something that existed at a particular time but is no longer. Therefore, they defined themselves as French by nationality and as Jewish by religion. The unity of "holy" which gave meaning to "people," and of "people" embodying the "holy," was destroyed. This division continues to this day. Even in the new State of Israel, which presumably exists to reunify the dispersed fragments of act, thought, and sentiment, discussion on this division continues.

Various movements in Jewish life such as Reform and Conservative Judaism, and Zionism aim to reconstitute this image. In fact, when we attempt to define "Jewishness," each of us seeks to give some kind of "oneness" and "wholeness" to himself.

Generally speaking, several approaches were used in the attempt to reconstitute the image or to regain "wholeness." One approach was the substitution of the part for the whole. In secular interpretations of Jewish life, "*nation*"—the ethnic or the culture group—becomes the whole. In religious interpretations, such as that of classic Reform Judaism, the religious element becomes the whole. Other interpretations aim at the reconstruction of Judaism by bringing "people" and "holy" together again. For instance, the Reconstructionist movement, by defining God in naturalistic categories, seeks to give new meaning to "people," customs, and *mitzvot* [commandments].

A difference remains. In the past, all we did, thought, and were related to the belief in a God who was master of the world. Our predicament today is that we have difficulties in recovering this faith. If we do not recover it, we cannot recover the "wholeness" which goes with Jewish experience.

IV

Thus we continue to ask ourselves, "What is a Jew?" It would have been difficult for my grandfather to define Judaism. He experienced it in the act. Every moment of the day was Jewish. Every moment of the day was human. He did not have to insist on kosher dishes. He just ate, and eating was inconceivable except from kosher dishes. . . . We express that which is human in that particular dialect of human experience which is American. He expressed that which was human in that particular dialect of human experience which was Jewish. It was the only one conceivable to him; it was the chosen one, the holy one.

We do not possess what he possessed; therefore we are searching. We construct verbal definitions of ourselves, yet they are not quite sufficient. What matters is not the word but the experience. I could describe what "love" is for hours —using all the dictionaries and the most sophisticated quotations from the world's great writers—yet we still would not know what love is. Those who know would find the description inadequate, because they possess the experience. Those who do not know would not quite grasp the meaning of it, for they lack the experience.

We are still in the verbal stage in our Jewishness. We must deepen our awareness of the importance of the act and of the thought. The crucial task for all of us is to attain that

wholeness which represents the reconstitution of our Jewishness in thought, act, and sentiment.

*Address delivered at the
National Hillel Summer
Institute, Camp B'nai B'rith,
Starlight, Pennsylvania,
September 3, 1958.*

There have always been Jews who, because of temper or temperament, have forsaken their faith for reasons real or imagined. Their numbers may have increased in recent years. But that is not crucial. What *is* crucial is the fact that there are thousands who, although never considering or condoning the way of the apostate, experience the same gnawing emptiness, the same perplexing questions, the same resentment of hollow faith and fate which have driven others to apostasy.

Weep not for those who go. Think rather of the living. Think of all those whose name and fate is *Jew*, who are perturbed by questioning, by doubts, by consuming emptiness, who have grown weary of an immortal name.

Think of the men and women, members of synagogues and temples, of lodges, societies and clubs, who in this hour can find in Judaism little explanation of either their human or Jewish predicaments. Think of them . . . the crisis of Judaism is within them.

Their questions recur with increasing persistency. The young keep asking their elders; the elders keep asking themselves. They get no answer, no vibrant life-giving affirmation of faith and fate equal to this moment in our history.

Modernity is holding Israel by the throat. He babbles but makes little sense. For he is unable to articulate clearly and distinctly the one word which gave coherence and meaning to his historic faith and fate. Without that word (unpronounceable now as in ancient days, but for different reasons) the historic image of Israel falls apart. I speak not only of the God of Israel—in the sense that Israel proclaimed Him, gave utterance to Him out of his vision of life, his experience with gods and men—but also of His special claim upon Israel because of His peculiar connection with the fate and faith of that tribe.

This God is central to an understanding of the historic conceptions of the Jews—of their conception of themselves and their neighbors, of their fate among the nations. No sociological account of the life and thought of the Jews is complete or valid without a recognition of the profound role played by their God, or their vision of God, in their attitude towards themselves and others.

Whatever the social, geographic, and economic factors that may have shaped their image of God, He is revealed in their thoughts as a power both tribal and universal, at once the God of Abraham, Isaac, and Jacob, and the God of the world—*a God who committed Israel to a particular function in a universal pattern.*

From unpublished notes, undated.

THE REDISCOVERY OF PURPOSE

At the conclusion of a recent Hillel Institute, I spoke to about two hundred student leaders of Hillel Foundations in the United States and Canada. I told them that I usually like to be a silent rabbi. I prefer to listen to what students say. I tell them it is from young people like themselves that I have learned much of what I know about the problems and concerns of Jewish youth in our time. Yet I am glad to be able to speak to you today. Yours is an unusual gathering. You come from many different places. You represent different organizations, different points of view about Jews and Judaism, and different attitudes toward life and society. Nevertheless, a common purpose has brought you here.

I know official purposes are important. But ultimately, people are not moved by them. Official purposes move people only as far as they are embodied in personal experience, in the life they lead. When there is a correspondence between official purpose and personal experience, you will find movement and will encounter an idea on the march.

An idea will march and become a movement only if it is intimately related to the living concerns of people, especially young people. The questions it stimulates and the answers it proposes must correspond to their needs. Hence I assume we have come to this gathering because something within us moved us to come. What this something is may not be entirely clear to all of us; it may be vague and tenuous, and we may be at a loss to explain it clearly to ourselves or to others.

Nevertheless, I believe we can all agree that, although many things separate us, we have one thing in common. We may differ on what we mean by such words as "Jewish people" or "God" or "revelation." These words can separate as well as unite. But there is at least one word we all have in common. If you wish, it is our *least* common denominator. If you wish, it is the most important fact about each of us and all of us together. The word is a name: Jew.

This name we share. It is our common heritage. It is a difficult name, both agonizing and exalting. It is a name with many meanings in history and theology, in literature and experience. You have heard rabbis, teachers, youth leaders, Jews, and Christians speak eloquently about the word and about the people, the religion and the culture of the Jews. The word Jew is woven inextricably into the texture of Western religion and thought, and the record of our history tells the story of the name we bear and the agonies associated with the name and the experience of Jews.

But what does the record mean? Indeed what can it mean, if I have not studied it and cannot respond to its meaning? What can its glory signify if it remains hidden from me and is not written in my own heart and my own experience?

There was a time in our history when the *historic* experience of the Jewish people and the [daily] experience of Jewish persons were closely related. In *Life Is with People*,[1] the authors use a sentence to characterize life in the "shtetl," the Eastern European Jewish townlet about which they write. The shtetl, they say, traces its descent from Sinai. The shtetl's

1. Mark Zborowski and Helen Herzog, *Life Is with People*, New York, 1953.

sense of descent from Sinai was not just a "fact" of history. It was part of the everyday experience of believing and non-believing Jews, of the learned and the ignorant alike. It was embodied in the texture of their collective and personal lives, in holiday observances and festival celebrations, in customs and ceremonies, in times of joy and of sorrow, in ways of speaking and ways of doing.

Our world differs vastly from that of the shtetl. Our acts and thoughts, our ways of speaking and doing and of being Jewish, are largely a reflection of the dominant culture in which our lives are cast. Even when we understand the meaning and implications of Sinai—and many of our people do not —we experience the fact of our being Jewish in a fragmentary way. We miss the historic dimension of Jewishness. The sense and experience of the Jewish past, which had been characteristic of Jewish life in the pre-modern period, has been reduced to the memory and experience of suffering. In the modern world, the name Jew derives its meaning largely from the experience of anti-Semitism in its various forms.

But a name which is merely a summary of remembered or experienced suffering is radically different from what the historic name *Jew* denotes—the religious and ethical ideas it represents, the poets and prophets it evokes, the world-shaping destiny that our forefathers and even the Christian world saw in it. Our Jewish experience has become one-dimensional; it is limited to the present tense. We say that we believe in, God and accept the Torah. But these terms have no compelling power; we have little knowledge to support their meaning. They have shallow roots and a limited time perspective.

I know the interest in Jews and Judaism among our young people has been growing. It may still be superficial, but it marks an important change in the attitudes of young people. Twenty or thirty years ago, the word *Jew* was, for many, merely a badge of shame, a source of self-consciousness, a reminder of foreign descent, a symbol of social and economic disadvantage.

These associations are fast disappearing. We have come to accept the name *Jew* as a natural, normal part of the American setting. Nevertheless, the word still lacks challenge. It sets no goals before us. Even among so-called "good Jews," Judaism and Jewishness have been reduced to attendance at meetings, an occasional visit to the synagogue, and the support of Jewish organizations. Do you wonder why the word *Jew* has retained an irritating connotation for many sensitive young Jews or why so many thoughtful Jews find themselves homeless in the magnificent synagogues and centers we have erected? They have not rejected Judaism; they have become indifferent to it. It has ceased to speak to their needs and innermost questions. They find challenge in Western-European thought and American culture, in the writers and artists who have become part of their lives. But what they know of Judaism, what they hear, see, and experience in the one-dimensional Jewish culture of our time is not attractive to them. And that which *might* speak to them is not accessible to them. They know little or nothing of the language, religion, and historic culture of the Jews. What has long passed for Jewish "education" in America consists largely of the repetition of a series of ritual words and phrases, some early Bible stories, a few customs, songs, and slogans.

Jewish education has failed to achieve what is, or ought to be, its major purpose. Jewish education, as I understand it, should equip us to extend and deepen our sense of kinship with other Jews in times past. It should help us to see our descent from Sinai as a contemporary event. It should heighten our sense of kinship and our affinity of spirit with Abraham and Jacob, with Yehuda Halevi and Maimonides, with the Baal Shem Tov and Theodor Herzl.

When I learn about Abraham, when I come to know and understand him, he comes to life again. Though belonging to the past, he becomes part of the living circle of friends, teachers, and guides who may affect and shape my life. Isaac, whom Abraham was ready to offer as a sacrifice to God, ceases to be a name in a biblical story far off in time and space and becomes flesh of my flesh and bone of my bone. So do Jeremiah and Job, Akiba and Yehuda Halevi, and many others like and unlike them. Priests and prophets, learned and untutored, wise and simple, saints and sinners—they all become part of my extended family. They speak to me and I to them. With some, I develop only a nodding acquaintance; to others, I feel very close. Their ways of life and thought— embodied in prose and poetry, in folk tales and proverbs, in prayer and admonition, in songs and stories—all these become part of the definition and meaning of the word *Jew*. The monosyllable becomes extended in time. It ceases to be limited to the present. It begins to gain in depth and color. It represents ideas and beliefs, persons and books, stories and chants, sorrows and joys. And I begin to sense what it means to trace one's descent from Sinai and to hope and pray for the return to Zion.

The word I have been trying to define is beginning to define itself. I still may be unable to capture the whole of my Jewish experience in one word or sentence. I still may be unable to summarize the diverse elements that enter into the making of Jewishness and Judaism in a neat statement. But I do *know* what it means to be Jewish. I am beginning to sense a relationship beyond words, between the record of Jewish history and my personal experience. The name *Jew* begins to give me a sense of direction, of goals, of purpose— Jewish and human.

I should like to emphasize these last two words—*Jewish, human*. I am frequently told that Jewish education must be designed to assure Jewish survival. But what about *human* survival? Jews are human beings. They fall in love not only as Jews. They suffer not only as Jews. They die not only as Jews. In this world there are not only Jewish problems. There are human problems and human predicaments. There is evil, injustice, and frustration. There is the threat of war and the fear of universal destruction. And there is the profound human need for roots, for faith, for hope. Jewish education must help us meet these needs. It must provide an answer to young people about the questions which perturb them—questions about love and sex, about evil and war, about illness and death. It must help them discover in Judaism guiding principles of thought and action for effective living as human beings, as Jews in this world.

Unfortunately, many of our young people make no demands upon Judaism. They are satisfied with little gifts and minor answers and find an Israeli folk song, a horah, or kosher delicatessen more appealing than the direction that Judaism might offer as a way of living and thinking in the modern world. The latter requires effort and study. It requires intelligent application and critical understanding. Above all, it requires a searching restlessness of mind and heart. Many of our young people seem to have lost this restlessness. They are too much in agreement with the goals of their parents, too satisfied with the material and cultural world of their parents. In this respect, they do not differ from American young people in general. Yet if Jewishness is to have meaning, it must stimulate within us a sense of restlessness, a dissatisfaction with things as they are, a seeking after the human values in Jewish tradition. We must go beyond parochial concerns and try to rediscover in Judaism what our forefathers found in it—a sense of role and purpose as Jews and as human beings.

This rediscovery of role and purpose calls for what I have defined as "self-extension in time." It also calls for a self-extension in space, a sense of relatedness to Jewish communities beyond our own community and borders. It calls for links with other Jews, for lines of communication, for leadership. It calls for intelligent and imaginative appreciation of the role of the Jews in Israel in the revitalization of Judaism in our day.

Most of all, however, it requires a decision on our part, as leaders of Jewish organizations, that the rediscovery of Judaism as a personally relevant experience is the most important task facing Jewish youth today. Without this decision we shall continue to repeat the clichés and slogans of the past, but we shall move neither ourselves nor others.

This task is more difficult than any in which we are now engaged. But it is our common task, the task on which we must all unite.

Keynote address, North-American Jewish Youth Conference, Camp B'nai B'rith, September 7, 1960.

In the dictionary of Jewish collective effort in the United States, the word "community" has become almost as popular as the historic word "synagogue." Yet it is almost as vague and undefined, and perhaps undefinable, as is the "God" of the synagogue. One might say that God and His community, the Jews, share a distinction. They both escape definition, but for opposite reasons. God escapes definition because He is too abstract; the Jews escape because they are too concrete.

When the word "organization" is put after "community," neither is simplified. The usual definition of community organization, whether as process or as field, are not very helpful. Add the word "Jewish" to both, and you are up against the Jewish problem—the historic predicament of the modern Jew which, in many of its aspects, is essentially a search for definition.

I

This search for definition is both a search to define the self and an attempt to define others. In either case, the search is not peculiar to Jews. But its intensity, the movements to which it has given birth, the feelings—expressed and repressed —it arouses, and the conflicts it engenders indicate that we are not dealing with an academic quest.

Each definition is often more a description of what Jews were or ought to be than what Jews are. Some modern definitions are more precise than others in the meaning of Jewish being historically and in our time, but almost all are meant to be prescriptions, guides to conduct, and programs for community effort designed to either enlarge or delimit the scope and perspective of Jewish community organization in America.

The several definitions of the word *Jew* or its adjective are crystallized in different concepts of Jewish community organization. Three such conceptions or proposals will be discussed: the Reconstructionist, the religionist, and the functional. Within each of these there are different emphases and variations.

I cannot, of course, deal with any or all of them in detail. I shall try to describe each position broadly and—I hope— objectively, comment on its scope and perspective, and conclude with several questions which may serve to stimulate discussion.

II

The Reconstructionist concept of Jewish community organization is contained in the term "organic community." This concept must be understood in the context of Reconstructionism's interpretation of Jewish history and tradition which conceives of Judaism as the evolving religious civilizations of the Jewish people.

"The term *civilization*," says Dr. Mordecai Kaplan, "is intended to stress that Judaism may be conceived variously." In so defining Judaism, the founder of the Reconstructionist movement attempts to describe the character of Jewish tradition and to provide a concept of Jewish community organization which will allow other definitions of Judaism to compete for recognition and influence.

But having suggested that the term "civilization" is meant to be an all-embracing term for divergent movements, ideas, and stages of Jewish development, Dr. Kaplan proceeds to qualify the word "civilization" with the word "religious." Religion is that which renders life worthwhile and gives it purpose and direction. Jewish religion is that quality in the individual and group life of Jews which "interprets the meaning of Jewish experience, and in the light of that meaning assigns to all aspects of the civilization, to all its institutional and cultural creations, their proper place in a hierarchy of values."

Since Judaism is an evolving religious civilization, past rigidities of creed and observance can and must be adjusted to meet the needs and wants of Jews in our time [say the Reconstructionists]. The organic community is designed to serve as the instrument for individual and collective experiences and expressions of Jewish civilization. It provides a common bond of relationship among all Jews—whatever their social, religious, or intellectual concerns—who share an interest in fostering Jewish group life.

Its basic principles are:

(1) the inclusion of all who desire to continue as Jews;

(2) the primacy of Jewish religious and educational institutions in the communal structure;

(3) the democratization of the community.

According to the Reconstructionists, a democratically elected community council should govern the activities of the community. The community council, rather than the different institutions in the community, should engage rabbis, teachers, artists, and social workers to serve those who wish to avail themselves of community services.

The spokesmen of Reconstruction feel that this pattern of organized Jewish life will enable Jews to experience a relationship to the total Jewish community rather than to the institutional segments with which they are now affiliated. It would make the claim of the Jewish community on the interests of Jews "prior and foremost over the claim of any institution or organization through which it [the community] functions."

III

When we examine the religionist approach, or the synagogue-centered concept of Jewish community, we discover few systematic statements on organization of the Jewish community along religious lines, even though Jewish religion and the synagogue have been the chief expressions of Jewish life. Issues of community organization have been discussed at rabbinical conferences, but these discussions have been largely in the nature of protests against secular encroachment on the synagogue, rather than concise formulations of objectives or carefully worked-out principles of community organization.

The synagogue representatives seem to realize that the Jewish community is not yet prepared to define the synagogue as the coordinating center of various communal agencies and institutions. Therefore, their major emphasis is on the need to infuse existing forms of communal effort with the spirit of Jewish religion, Jewish learning, and respect for Jewish tradition, and they advocate rabbinical participation in community planning.

Henry Hurwitz's recent proposals (in *The Menorah Journal*) are merely variants of this religious approach. He too proposes to make religion the primary source of Jewish identification and institutional expression. While he envisions ultimate organization of the total Jewish community along religious lines, he first calls for coordination of diverse religious groups. Thus the role of religion can be articulated more effectively, and its influence can become proportionate to its numbers and place in Jewish history and in present-day Jewish life.

IV

The functional approach to Jewish community organization provides the rationale—stated or implied—for most of the community councils, federations, and welfare funds. Although their structure and specific functions may vary from community to community, they are agreed that the primary objective of Jewish community organization is the coordination of Jewish community effort for maximum service, efficiency, and economy in the interests of "the general welfare" of Jews.

This position is dominantly pragmatic in character. Its ultimate goal is *total* community organization. However, its scope at any given time is defined by whatever is possible under given local conditions—centralized fund raising, allocation, and social services, if that is all the community interest will permit at a particular time; education, if possible; civic defense, if agreement among competing or overlapping agencies can be reached.

This approach seeks neither to define Jews nor to choose between definitions. It is concerned with coordination and accommodation of various activities of Jews, regardless of their ideological sources. It would speak for all Jews where there is consensus. It would allow for individual expression (by its constituent groups) where basic ideological conflict is likely to destroy the unity already achieved.

The functional position differs fundamentally from the other two approaches which have their center in a time perspective and a historic orientation. For Dr. Kaplan as well as for religionists, the Jewish community—whatever its variations and divergencies from the historic past—is or should be an expression of the Jews' historic civilization and religion. The Jewish community can be defined as Jewish only if it is seen as an extension in time and space of the historic entity known as the Jewish people.

Without this historic interrelationship, one cannot define what *Jewish* means or what Jewish needs are. The organization of the Jewish community is meant to strengthen the relationship of Jews to their historic past, thus helping them discover criteria for authentic Jewish expression.

V

In the light of this relationship to history, religionists and Reconstructionists alike can set up a value system to measure the claims of the activities and institutions in today's Jewish community. Thus, Dr. Kaplan and the religionists insist upon the primary claim of Jewish religion, education, and creative effort over the interest and budgets of community organization.

But it is precisely at this point, say the functionalists, that the religionists and Reconstructionists fail to meet the reality of Jewish diversity—ideological, religious, social, economic—and its institutional expressions. The introduction of historic purpose and goals as decisive factors in determining the objectives (or ends) of Jewish community organization inevitably introduces the problem of definition and interpretation—divisive rather than uniting elements in contemporary Jewish life. Since voluntary consent of diverse groups to work together is the precondition of centrally organized Jewish community effort, it becomes necessary to limit the objectives and scope of Jewish community organization at any given moment to the task of securing unity wherever and whenever possible.

The time perspective of this approach is, therefore, largely the present and the measurable future. It articulates no valuation as to historic purpose, either past or future. It does not definitely affirm—even though many of its adherents believe in it—Jewish survival as an objective of Jewish community effort.

The focus of its concerns is with Jewish needs or, in most instances, with the needs and interests of Jews as they express themselves both in the present state of community development and in the foreseeable future.

The rationale of this approach stems largely from the profession from which community organization has generally emerged: social welfare. Its tools are dominantly the methods of social research, the community survey, and the social study. These provide guides and sanctions for proposed changes in the pattern and function of institutional life.

This does not mean, however, that the exponents of the functional approach are unaware of, or unresponsive to, the claims of Jewish history and tradition. However, these claims —as embodied in Jewish religion, education, and culture—are not given an a priori or presupposed primacy, as in the proposed programs of the religionists and Reconstructionists. Although there is evidence of growing interest in Jewish education and culture within functionally organized Jewish communities, the response to the claims of these historically oriented efforts varies with the character of the community organization and with the extent of Jewish knowledge and sympathy among its lay and professional leadership.

The claims of history and tradition—as reflected in Jewish religion and education—become compelling at a budget committee meeting only when they are seen as needs and desires of Jewish individuals and groups. They can share or hope to share in the Jewish community's services and budgets only by articulating their needs and making appropriate demands on the Jewish community.

Martin Cohn summarizes the functionalist rebuttal to what I have called the historically oriented approaches: "Fundamentally, community organization must be an expression of community culture, and culture cannot be organized. Judgments as to the possible types of community organization which might be effective relate to judgments as to the level of development of a community's culture."

This statement raises as many questions as it answers. A clarification of the objectives of Jewish community organization requires an answer to such questions as:

(1) What is the function of both the lay and professional leader in giving direction to the development of community culture?

(2) What is the role of Jewish history and tradition in determining the direction?

(3) Is there a way of reconciling the functional- and historically oriented approaches to Jewish community organization?

Delivered as part of Oneg Shabbat program on "Directions in Jewish Community Organization," General Assembly of Council of Jewish Federations and Welfare Funds, Cincinnati, Ohio, December 10, 1949.

THE AMERICAN JEWISH COMMUNITY:
WHAT'S AHEAD?

Even though I was invited to discuss the future of the American Jewish community, I must reject the implication that I can prophesy or predict the future. Predictions must be based on scholarly research, and prophecy should be buttressed or validated by some superscription such as "Thus said the Lord, the God of Israel," as is done in the Bible.

I am not equipped to make predictions on the basis of scientific studies supported by the requisite number of graphs and statistical tables. And even if Jeremiah himself were to appear in the American Jewish community today and say: "Thus said the Lord, the God of Israel," I am not sure he would be believed. People did not believe him in his own time either, although for different reasons, and they claimed that his words were not God's words. The predicament of the Jew today is in his uncertainty as to who can speak in the name of God or whether there is a God. Having said this, I almost have stated the fundamental problem facing Jewish community life.

However, even though I have no graphs or statistics about Jews, I have a great deal of contact with Jews. More specifically, I have contact with many Jews whom one rarely meets in the Jewish community. I meet them in the universities—

students and graduate students, scholars, librarians, and professors. They rarely belong to our community, and if they do belong, they seldom attend meetings. They are influencing the life of the American Jewish community in many ways. Yet even when they join a synagogue or communal institution, they hardly ever employ their knowledge and intelligence to help us improve the Jewish community. Occasionally they attend religious services. Quite often they want their children to become Bar Mitzvah or confirmed, and so they send them to Hebrew school. But in their world of ideas and intellectual concerns, in the lectures they deliver and in the books they write, Judaism is either peripheral or not discernible.

Their distance from Jewish life is essentially due to their feeling that the Jewish community has little or no room for them. Their intellectual interests are out of place at men's clubs and sisterhood meetings, in the Bar Mitzvah-centered worship of the synagogue, and in the numerous "activities" of our communal organizations. Some have established a relationship with the Jewish community or have achieved a sense of at-homeness in it, yet they frequently echo the sentiments expressed by Evelyn Rossman in *Commentary* some time ago:

> I go to Temple and don't pray. I light candles on Friday night but don't observe the Sabbath. I contribute to Israel but I do not share the faith of my Israeli friend that only superior people live in Israel. I support a Jewish Youth Center, but I'm opposed to Jewish boy scouts and Jewish basketball teams. . . . I teach my own children the prayers and blessings that my father taught to me, though I haven't said them since my own childhood. . . . Perhaps I shall some day be able to say "No" to the voice on the telephone that pleads, "Could you help us out just this time? I've called dozens of

people. I can't find anyone else. . . ." But when it's time to say *No*, I lack the courage . . . I do not want, even now, to separate myself from the community, but cannot find a way to feel at home in it; or a way to live a Jewish life that is not submerged in trivialities. I know, however, that many people depend upon the activities that I can't bear, and that they fulfill some need I don't have.[1]

Mrs. Rossman expresses her predicaments more vigorously and emphatically than do many other Jews who accept their membership in Jewish organizations quite naturally, in fact so naturally that they tend to become indifferent to the meaning and implications of their membership. Nevertheless, neither the mushrooming membership lists of our synagogues nor the enormous increase in Jewish school enrollment and attendance nor the multiplicity of projects of Jewish organizations that constitute the texture of American Jewish life can conceal the fact that there are numerous people who share the felings of Mrs. Rossman and of the university professors I have mentioned.

One does not need to be a university teacher or a student to sense the emptiness and hollowness, the superficiality and more-than-occasional vulgarity that dominate much of Jewish communal life. American Jews have settled down to a kind of Judaism that demands little and offers little in return. The middle-class character of the American Jewish community has emerged clearly. The forms and patterns of Jewish existence are now deeply rooted in modern American experience. Some Israelis still may wonder whether American Jews will survive as Jews. But I think we can take for granted that we will survive for a long time. We have developed a formula for our integration into American society.

1. Evelyn Rossman, "Judaism in Northrup," *Commentary*, November, 1957, pp. 390-391.

We define ourselves as a faith group, as a religion. We may be religious more in sentiment than in content. Nevertheless, this self-definition is in harmony with the dominant American attitude which accepts the validity of religious pluralism and supports America's traditional affirmation of freedom of religion.

This formula has made Jewish identity in America acceptable. It is respectable. It is secure. It is an authentic ingredient of American society.

Moreover, our sense of at-homeness in America is fortified by the security that springs from a sense of achievement. Ours is a significant record of achievement. The image of generosity which the Jewish community has created—its dynamic organizational structure, its response to human needs here and abroad, its phenomenal rise from immigrant beginnings to a position of economic, political, and intellectual prominence in American society and world Jewry—all of this rightfully merits respect and admiration.

Nevertheless, the individual frequently seems lost and overlooked in the organizational activities and projects of our community. We attend numerous meetings in which we discuss problems and needs of our community, yet somehow we fail to ask the questions which are fundamental to these discussions: What is the character of Jewish group life and what significance does it have for the life of human-beings-born-Jews? What is the place of a Jewish person in the Jewish community? What should a Jew derive from his membership in the Jewish community besides the satisfaction from activities in which he engages? What does he do with his solitude when he does not attend a meeting or solicit support for some Jewish cause? Must he always *do* something in order to be Jewish?

The machinery of Jewish community life is running at full speed. All of us are constantly "busy," engaged in various community projects. We support our projects and distinctive Jewish institutions because we feel they are needed to help us maintain our distinctive identity as Jews in the modern world. Yet we have not really begun to face the fundamental question that has confronted Jews and Judaism ever since their emancipation and entry into the modern world: What is the ultimate meaning of Jewish difference?

This question was not asked by the Jews of the ghetto. They knew precisely why they were different and what the nature of the difference was. Their self-image was clear. It was shaped by their faith in a God whose plan called for one nation, His chosen people which, although dispersed throughout the world, would worship Him everywhere. The Jews' dispersion among the nations and their distinctive ways of thinking and doing were part of a divine plan that would ultimately lead to their personal and collective salvation. This plan gave meaning and purpose to their lives. Above all, it gave them a sense of purpose and role in the world. Their community structure and the way of life they managed to create within the confines of the ghetto reflected their awareness of this role. Often, they found God's way quite difficult, but they also found it to be good. Their way of life was structured by the Ten Commandments and was woven together by the fellowship of like-minded Jews, a community-wide system of education, and the shared beauty of holidays and festivals. They found purpose and joy in their identity. And they knew what they were. Their speech and gestures, their ways of eating and drinking, the way they dressed and worked and prayed and rested—they all reflected and expressed the fact of their Jewish being.

Spatially the ghetto was separated from its neighbors. It had a boundary line that kept Jews and non-Jews apart. In addition to the boundary line, however, there also was what I like to call a "gatekeeper" who enforced the separation. If a city has a boundary line but no gatekeeper, you have freedom of mobility—you can move whenever you want to. The ghetto had both a boundary line and a gatekeeper, the [gate-keeper being the] various forces—pressures of the non-Jewish majority, governmental edicts, municipal laws, and similar factors—which prevented the Jews from moving into the non-Jewish world.

However, even though the Jews of the ghetto could not move in space, they were able to move in time. Everything the Jew did related him to time—it related him to Sinai; it related him to creation; it related him to Abraham, Moses, and Jacob. He got up in the morning, washed his hands, and recited the appropriate benediction. The benediction was a link in time to the source of all life. On his way to the synagogue, he met another Jew, and walking together they became involved in a discussion of some talmudic passage. Suddenly, Rabbi Akiba, who had lived around 130 C.E. [Common Era], became a contemporary. They were talking as if they knew him personally. They quoted him and argued about him. He was one of them. Tradition was a contemporary experience. The two men entered the synagogue and began to pray in that particular intonation which had been handed down from generation to generation—from time immemorial, as far as they were concerned.

Whether on weekday, Sabbath, or holiday, the language and music of prayer made the past contemporaneous and reminded them of time—of patriarchs, prophets, and scholars. On Passover, Elijah would come and visit them. In their *succot*,[2] during the harvest festival, they had a special way of welcoming Abraham, Isaac, and Jacob to their table and observance. They went beyond space into time. They had a means of locomotion in time because their way of life linked past and present. The difficult and often tragic life of the ghetto became transmuted by an association with the great spokesmen of Jewish tradition. This extension in time gave

2. Temporary huts erected by Orthodox Jews in observance of the festival of Succot.

Jews a sense of at-homeness in a much wider world and provided them with resources of life and thought which enabled them to survive. But they were concerned with more than mere physical survival. They were living for something that was heaven-bound, for a way of life that gave meaning and purpose to their existence as Jews and provided an answer to their predicament and concerns as human-beings-born-Jews.

We do not possess the same sense of purpose and meaning. Most Jewish discussions today tend to end with the question, "What is a Jew?" One can of course define what a Jew is. Yet no study can answer what I consider to be the essential question: Will it be satisfying to be a Jew? Does being Jewish give us a sense of the parochial and the limited, or does it link us with forces, personalities, and ideas that can change us—that will not merely help us survive but will provide an answer to our problems as human beings? The major predicament of Jewish life in our time arises precisely from the fact that it is earthbound. It is no longer limited in space. In fact, ever since the Emancipation, Jews have conquered the world of space. Yet in the process they lost their sense of time, their connection with the roots of their life and thought. As a result, they no longer have an understanding of their history. Occasionally they even want to reject it.

For example, a well-known Jewish musician once endorsed the aims of the Free Land Movement which sought to establish a Jewish homeland, not in Israel but in Australia. It would be good for the Jews to start afresh, without the burdens of the past, he said.

To some Jews, the nature of Jewish experience in the past constitutes a genuine burden. To many others, the past is not even a burden. We do not possess it. It is not ours, for we know little or nothing about it. Not knowing our history, we really have no history.

Therefore our Jewishness is limited. It possesses a space

dimension, but no time dimension. As a result, we have no adequate answer to the question, "What is a Jew?" For if you have no time dimension, you do not have the fundamental Jewish orientation which is implicit in Jewish history—that sense of purpose and of role which motivated Jews in the past. They knew why they were living in this world.

Having lost this sense of role as well as the mechanism for its discovery, Jews today are limited in time. Yet we cannot be saved by space alone. We cannot be saved by walls or gate keepers. Nor shall we find an answer to our problems by relating ourselves to the Jews of Israel, as some of our leaders advocate. The State of Israel still provides what is largely a spatial solution. It has not, or not yet, been able to resolve the conflict between space and time and to integrate the past with the present. Many young Israelis reject time and want to begin history anew—with a new nation and a new tradition divorced from two thousand years of history; this merely signifies martyrdom, cowardice, a failure of the national will. Therefore they, too, reject time and thus confront the problem of having to discover an answer to the question, "What is a Jew?"

Our difficulty is that we have tried to answer this question only in the present tense and in terms of spatial relationships. Such an approach, however, can clarify the meaning of our Jewish identity as little as it can clarify my identity as a person. If, in answer to the question, "What am I?" you were to define me solely in terms of what I am at this very moment, you could never really define me. A person is a continuum which begins on the day of his birth and, indeed, antedates his birth. Similarly, a Jew cannot be defined except in terms of a historic context, that is, in a time dimension. When I speak of "time dimension" I am not referring to a detached academic investigation. I do not suggest you read a number of history books and distill what you have read into a definition. Time dimension is experience. You begin to sense your own link with the past—with Abraham, Isaac, and Jacob, with Moses, Jeremiah, and Spinoza, with good and bad Jews, with lowly and wealthy Jews, with saints and sinners. They all are part of our history, and a meaning for Jewish life and Jewish experience in our time can emerge only as we develop a relationship with them.

A conclusion seems inescapable. If our Jewish community wants to rediscover its primary purpose—if it wants to begin to sense that it is not merely a speck on the sands of time but has a beginning, roots, and a future—the program of Jewish education must be reshaped. Jewish education once again must help us discover the means of traveling in time.

American secular education does this for American children. When we study Lincoln or the Civil War, when we read Jefferson or the Federalists, when we delve into American literature and read about the heroes of American folklore, we have a means of locomotion in time. As we think about these men, read a book, or see a flag, we are reminded of the past and we sense a relationship to it. It is linked with our life. It becomes part of our life.

For several reasons, Jewish education does not do the same for us. All too often, it is flimsy and shallow. We do not give it enough time to discover time. The National Study on Jewish Education has shown how little Jewish education our children really get, even though the great majority may attend some Jewish school at one time or another.

Insufficient time for Jewish education is one problem. A second problem is that the purpose of Jewish education in the United States is often a kind of group therapy. You send your youngsters to a Jewish school because it will facilitate their adjustment in a hostile world. Jewish education is preventive therapy so that they will know who they are in case they encounter prejudice or are exposed to other manifestations of group hatred. Many community leaders (including religious leaders) advocate the rationale that Jewish education will make for group survival. We are troubled by the fear of intermarriage. This fear is what makes many parents send their children to Hebrew school. We must create pleasant Jewish experiences for our children so that they will remember that it is pleasant to be Jews and will not break away from the group and its institutions.

The education we offer in our schools is therapy education, survival education, pleasantness education. Such emphases may do until a child reaches the age of twelve or thirteen. But pleasantness is not enough to answer his questions when he leaves school and enters college. As he studies philosophy, anthropology, or sociology, he begins to encounter some of man's most persistent and profound questions—his questions about God and man and the relationship between man and man. He begins to discover the answers of some of the other great traditions of the world. What does Judaism have to say to him about these questions? Is Judaism designed to answer the questions of man as man? Other traditions seem to offer an answer, but the Judaism he knows does not.

We must go beyond group survival as the chief purpose of Jewish education. Indeed, we must transform Jewish education into something which extends beyond the walls of the school and challenges the entire community.

The Hillel Foundation at the University of Chicago annually conducts a Maccabean festival in the beautiful university chapel. It is a major event on campus. The chapel carillons play Chanukkah music. Jews from all over the city attend the program. Yet every year we face a dilemma as we begin to plan the program. What should be its nature? For instance, what musical selections should we use? I am familiar with Israeli folk dances and songs, and I like many of them. But they are hardly great music. And I often ask myself what the Jewish community has done to stimulate the creation of something of which intelligent and sensitive

Jews can say, "This is mine, and I enjoy it. This is something which links me in time." Has any Jewish community, for instance, commissioned a great musician to compose a new Chanukkah oratorio so that we shall have something besides Handel's *Judah Maccabaeus?* As it plans a mass event in conjunction with an annual UJA appeal or Bonds for Israel campaign to which artists from all over the world may be invited, has any of our large communities ever given thought to the possibility of sponsoring an equally impressive Passover festival for which it would commission a Passover cantata or oratorio—something that would enhance Jewish culture, enrich the culture of the United States and the musical world, and give us something in our solitude—a tune I can retain and carry with me as I walk home from the concert or as I travel on a train somewhere far away?

The Jewish community must begin to think of Jewish education not as education for parochialism or survival, but as education for life, for answering the problems of human beings who were born Jews and who, as human beings, are not different from their neighbors. We must bring Jewish tradition out into the open as one of the great traditions of the Western world. We must express it spiritually and aesthetically in the various dimensions possible in our time so that its answers and commitments will become implicit in the lives we lead, the things we do, the institutions we establish, and the community we create.

Membership in the community I have described would be more than an act of membership in the present or in a particular synagogue or particular organization at a particular time. It would be membership in a community which reflects an affirmation and experience of relationships, no matter how tenuous, beyond this place and beyond this time to other times and other places, to the historic experience and creative expression which we designate as Jewish tradition.

Thus conceived, the community is more than the sum of

concrete living and visible persons labeled Jews at any given time. It includes the invisible Moses and Akiba, Hillel and Shammai, Yehuda Halevi and A. D. Gordon, Louis Brandeis and Stephen S. Wise. It includes a host of others like them and unlike them, as objects of emulation or as subjects of dissent. They all are members of the Jewish community which I am describing, as symbols, ideas, and unconscious influences. And as such they have a voice in our community's life and form.

But we must be able to hear and see them. Therefore it is for us to create the instruments which will enable us to make their voices heard and their faces seen—which will link the past with the present and establish the linkage which will assure the future.

Presented at Young Men's Service Group, Jewish Community Council of Essex County, Newark, New Jersey, June 3, 1959.

On Israel

Part 2

and American Jewry

I

October 3, 1950

Although it is only two weeks since we landed in Haifa and about ten days since we arrived in Jerusalem, it seems like many months—so many impressions, so many people, so many conversations, so much searching and self-searching in the short time since we left New York. . . .

Everyone has been very friendly. Everyone has offered to help—we have been received cordially, as persons. But the idea I came with, the object of my visit, is not yet fully understood. And I find myself in the rather unpleasant position of having to justify my coming, especially since I cannot produce the $500,000 I should have come with. As soon as I got on the boat I was met by skepticism: "How much of a budget do you have?" In less direct and more refined ways, people have emphasized the importance of a physical plant worthy of B'nai B'rith and the American Jewish community. In the words of a former president of [Israel's] Students Organization, "It's got to be better, much better than what the students could do for themselves in physical facilities, programming, and the rest." The present head of the Students Organization put it this way: "You've got to begin with a 'bombshell.' "

By "bombshell," he meant that there must be enough in your physical facilities and program the moment you begin, to counteract the suspicions attached to your being an American agency. You will be suspected anyway, but you may as well have the advantages of American organization—begin with a bang! The physical facilities must be spacious, attractively furnished, inviting. You must have a rich and varied library in many languages, newspapers from all over the world, a library of phonograph recordings, recreational facilities, a kitchen. And you must have a full program—something every day.

II

October 15, 1950

By far the most stimulating and exciting session I have had was with Martin Buber. Although I had met him about a week before and exchanged a few words with him, it was with awe and trepidation that I came to his home. I found my usual technique of questioning my interlocutor was failing me, as the master of the *I and Thou* insisted, gently but persistently, on turning the tables on me. Until I met him, I managed to make people tell me what *they* thought Hillel should do at the [Hebrew] University, what students required, what people expected Hillel to do, and the like. But the gentle and wise Martin Buber wanted to know what *I* had come for. I kept telling him that the program of the Foundation was to emerge from the needs and interests of the students here, and that my main task in these early weeks of my stay was to discover the nature of the university, the students, and the community. But all to no avail. He admitted this was a necessary and wise procedure, but kept pushing me to tell him what my ultimate objective was. Of course, he remarked, a club-house would be useful. But not sufficiently important. He broke down my resistance. I admitted the failure of my position as the leader in the dialogue, and proceeded to unfold for him my conception of the purpose and function of Hillel at the Hebrew University. He listened attentively to my analysis of the problem, to my concept of program, and he seemed to be quite pleased. He then began to expand some of my thoughts, and concluded: "I shall be glad to help in any way I can."

According to Buber's analysis of the problem of Jewish youth in this country, the Hillel Foundation must help in recapturing the meaning of Jewish tradition, the consciousness of the *living* God, the *renewal* of the biblical awareness of man in relationship with the divine and in search of the divine. The basic function of the Hillel Foundation is therefore spiritual, and its program must be devised to create an atmosphere conducive to self-discovery and to the discovery of other selves in a common search. Basic to this program is not a house but a person—or rather persons—who by the contagion of their personal integrity, quest, and direction can stimulate others and lead to the formation of intimate groups of activity.

"You will have to have a house," he said, "but that is not enough. What you need is, I emphasize, a garden, because in a garden you are more likely to chat than to argue. The great curse here is that everybody argues, and in an argument the objective is not the common quest for the truth, but rather the sharpening of one's position to overcome the opponent. What we need is conversation rather than debating and arguing."

One may or may not agree with Buber's specific emphasis. What was important to me was the encouragement of my concept of Hillel as more than a club-house, physical center, or extracurricular leisure time activity. The first person to speak to me of Hillel's purpose in such terms was Simon Halkin, whose concept [of Hillel] grows out of an analysis of the needs of Israel youth. For him, as for Martin Buber, the great danger here is that our youth may become alienated in time and space (Halkin's phrase) from the historic Jewish past and from world Jewry. Hillel's program must be directed toward increasing the students' knowledge of the Jewish heritage, of the problems and concerns of Jews in our time. Like Buber, he emphasized, as is clear to all of us who work in Hillel, that our direction must be *implied* in our program and must not be articulated as creed or slogan. In other words, the group atmosphere we create will be a determining factor. The factors which make up group atmosphere are not easily discovered. But it is generally agreed that the kind of building we shall have, and the physical set-up in the building—the library, the music room, the furnishings—will affect the atmosphere. This applies equally to the program. Whether we emphasize the purely social aspects and physical comforts—or begin immediately to develop a cultural program of high quality—will be exceedingly important.

I must confess though that in the midst of the students' needs for housing, food, and clothing, the discussion of Hillel's purpose beyond the physical is exceedingly difficult. Last night Nell [Mrs. Pekarsky] and I spent about three hours with Professor Reiffenberg, dean of the natural sciences. Like so many others he dwelt on the physical needs of the students. Although we shall not be able to provide dormitories, it is clear that our building will have to be comfortable and pleasant, an escape from the dreariness of the students' physical surroundings.

III

December 25, 1950

I appreciate your desire to know all about the problems and predicaments, the personal as well as the official, of a Hillel director away from home. It is true that we have avoided references to our personal life here, except insofar as the personal has been official. In the life of a Hillel director and his family, at home or abroad, so much of one's private life is Hillel life that the two quite often become one. And it is rather difficult to tell whether the institution is an extension of the person or the person an extension of the institution.

Nell and I see little point to dwelling on the difficulties of our everyday life in Israel. Nor do we see any point to reporting on those *tzores*—or rather *tzarot* [anguish], although this is an altogether different kind of *tzores*—to which all flesh, as flesh, is heir whether in Israel or in the States. And to consider illness an accident of geography rather than the will of God would be as ungracious as it is incorrect.

This much needs to be said: It is difficult to understand the climate of our work here, the nature of the problems of the students and the university, and their relationship to each other without actually experiencing these things. It would be difficult for me to communicate adequately the *American predicament* of Jewish students from the United States without giving the impression that I am playing an old record on the personality adjustment of Jewish students *in America* and applying it to American students in Israel. Yet that is the record I keep hearing.

Some time ago, about twenty-five American students gathered at our home. It was a social evening, with home-baked cakes from Nell's cupboard, American coffee and tea, long-playing records, and conversation. Although it was intended as a purely social evening, so many students kept asking me questions about Hillel that the social hour soon turned into a question-and-answer period. These were some of the questions put to me: Why Hillel in Jerusalem? Why should Hillel, an American organization, do it? Do you intend to bring Judaism or Jewish culture to the Israelis? Isn't Hillel likely to segregate the American students at the Hebrew

University? And if you are going, as you say, to serve all students, why have this tea for American students?

But more important than the questions was the atmosphere of fear that seemed to permeate the questions, and the total absence of a sense of the worthwhileness of the American heritage and its possible contribution to the life of Israel. Here were Americans without a sense of the meaning of their American experience, living in the image which so many Israelis have that all that Americans can contribute is money.

I pulled a Pekarsky on them—I encouraged a dialogue. They talked and I asked casual questions, in the hope of clearing up the misconceptions and prejudices of my *landsmanshaft*. I was not surprised to hear their questions. I had expected them, and soon after my arrival I had been told of the lively discussions of the subject of Hillel among the American students. It was good to have them talk about it freely, now in my presence. Before the evening was over they asked me, "When are you going to get a house? How long will we have to wait? The Israelis need it badly; they need a common meeting place, and we need it too." Of course suspicions, long nurtured, are not easily dissipated. Ultimately, by our works they will know us. But before they left, they seemed eager for Hillel to begin in its own house and eager to cooperate.

More important than the attitude of the Americans—although their attitude is important insofar as it affects Israelis—is the attitude of the Israelis. The problems that are likely to arise from their attitudes center largely about their lack of experience with extra-curricular activities, their political commitments, and their inability to understand a non-political student center, their suspicion of an American-supported agency, and their fear of Hillel's possible competition with the *Histadrut Hastudentim* (the Students Organization). That a student center is necessary is an unquestioned proposition. But can it be nonpolitical? Can anything be nonpolitical in the atmosphere of sharp partisanship permeating the educational, economic, religious life of this country? Every party has its youth movement, and as you walk into Terra Sancta you see the posters of the *studentim leumiyim* representing the Heruth group; those of Yavneh, the religious adherents; and of Mapai [Labor Movement] and Mapam [Labor-Communist Movement], each of these student groups meeting for the most part in the headquarters of the parent organizations.

IV

September 27, 1953

As I think back upon my correspondence and reports I often hear a voice of lamentation, at times loud, more often suppressed, being heard in Zion. Occasionally, the voice of the turtle is heard in the land, and I sing my own song of songs: the significance and the perhaps historic meaning of Hillel in Jerusalem. This song may have been stimulated by a conversation with a student, by a discussion on Jewish religion, or by the hushed silence of students, seated on the floor in my home, listening to Bach. In these acts and experiences, a Foundation has its real being.

Let me, therefore, supplement my recent reports by describing some of the human aspects of our work here.

I have always considered it the ultimate task of a Hillel director to transmute institutional activity into personal relationship. In the growing institutionalism of our society—its educational and religious bodies included—the personal bond between director and student is, I believe, the significant factor in Hillel's education of Jewish persons. And I have tried to work in the spirit of this belief. In this I have been helped by the conditions of work on the campuses I came to. When I began at Cornell twenty years ago, the Foundation had no house of its own. The "home away from home" had of necessity to be a relationship between student and director rather than a physical space. So it was during my first two or three years at Northwestern and, later, in the early days, at the University of Chicago. So it has been during the last three years at the Hebrew University in Jerusalem.

I have not considered our houselessness, here or in the States, as homelessness. But I have found our lack of quarters here in Jerusalem particularly trying, once we reached the stage where personal relationships required breathing space. In any case, the campus situation here called for a decided emphasis on a personal relationship of the director with students. Here was a new institution, new in name, concept, and approach, coming to a country and student body sharply divided politically and religiously, deeply suspicious of non-political or nonpartisan platforms, especially those of foreign lineage. We needed to understand the students and be understood by them.

Our home has become the base of our activity. We take every occasion to invite students and to encourage professors to refer them to us. Our doors are wide open, day and night, weekday and holiday. The fame of my wife's chocolate cake has spread from Dan to Beersheba and beyond there to Boston, "if not higher."

Out of these meetings with students have developed personal relationships, mutual confidence, and often ties of friendship. Ends in themselves, they are at the same time elements of self-education and orientation for the director and are essential factors in the organic growth of the Foundation at the Hebrew University. They suggest the role and function of Hillel in the university community.

I have met students or have made contact with them in many other ways. They come seeking advice regarding their studies here or in the United States, opportunities for part-time work, scholarships, loans, books. Almost invariably they conclude the interview with requests for help in these matters.

We have tried to help. With the cooperation of Hillel directors on several campuses, a number of students preparing to study at American universities have secured lodging, part-time work, and scholarships. American B'nai B'rith groups and personal friends have sent us food packages or scrip certificates which enable us to assist some students. Israel's B'nai B'rith lodges have helped us secure employment and home hospitality for students. Hadassah has provided special medical and convalescent care to some students. And a local physician, a teacher in the university's medical school, has offered us free medical attention for indigent students. . . .

Many students at the Hebrew University come from out of town. But the Americans are farthest away from home. They may have felt close to Israel prior to their arrival, yet soon after they reach Jerusalem they usually find themselves in need of guidance and orientation.

Here, for instance, is a student from Minnesota, a youthful and eager chap. He knows no Hebrew but wants to study at the University. He needs a room but cannot pay much. And what he needs most is to make some friends, especially Israeli ones.

And here is another American, precocious and sickly. Starved physically and emotionally, he needs immediate medical care and someone friendly to talk to.

Now the telephone is ringing . . . it's the Hadassah Hospital. A student by the name of John M. has just been brought to the hospital from the Old City of Jerusalem, in Jordan. He is sick. His rabbi gave him my name before he left for the Middle East. . . .

And here is a cable from a mother concerned about her son. Will I check why he has not written in six weeks?

On her way from Jordan as a member of the Lafayette College tour, Catherine M. stops in Jerusalem. A casual meeting turns into several counseling sessions. Shall she marry him or not? She is Christian—he is Jewish. She was hoping Israel would help her make up her mind.

And here's a letter from a rabbi in California about the Christian girl who came to see me ten days ago. She had met an Israeli student while both were at college. After their marriage they came to Tel Aviv. Now her husband has left her. She needs a counselor, perhaps a psychiatrist. Can I help her? And I must check on her lawyer—is he reliable?

And there is that cable from Michigan: "J. B. with polio in government hospital near Haifa. Check on medical care. Arranging passage."

All this is part of the work of the Hillel director, here as in the United States. But here there is an added international dimension and the awful sense of guardianship and responsibility as a two-way communication center across the seas.

Each case requires careful consideration, sympathetic listening, a judicious response, and the cooperation of experts on whose judgment the director must rely. Letters, cables, telephone calls, and out-of-town travel, time, and money. . . .

I trust this report has given you some idea how and where a Hillel director without a Hillel house does his work. But, I am glad to add, the building is ready. All we need is furniture. It is not likely that the house will be completely furnished by the time school begins. But we are going to begin activities in the house, even if only partly furnished. The students at the university need the house, and the Foundation needs it to develop the program fully and effectively.

V

September 8, 1955

During my five years in Israel I have increasingly come to realize that the function of the Hillel Foundation at the Hebrew University is not really unlike that of the Hillel Foundation at the University of Chicago or anywhere else in the world. For essentially, the problems which young Israelis face are the same questions which concern young Jews everywhere—the questions about God, man, the Jewish state, and the meaning of their Jewish identity. The accident of geography may affect the context of the questions but not their ultimate effect.

It is in this spirit that *Beit Hillel* [Hillel House] has tried to function in Israel. People have gradually come to understand that this is not just a student center or building providing facilities for youth activities, but an institution concerned with the ultimate questions of Jewish life.

Among the programs which I wanted to initiate in pursuit of this goal was a series of discussions by visiting lecturers from outside Israel. Rabbi Morris Adler of Detroit happened to be in Israel just at that time, and I invited him to deliver the opening lecture on "Religious Trends in American Judaism." He accepted. But when I discussed my plan with some young Israeli friends, they suggested that I eliminate the word "religious" and merely announce the topic as "Trends in American Judaism." They felt Israeli students were more likely to respond to something that did not include the word "religious."

I decided to take a chance and announced the topic as we had originally planned it. However, I felt it would be prudent to anticipate the possibility of failure, and I therefore had the room arranged to provide an intimate, home-like atmosphere even if only a handful of people were to show up.

More than a hundred people came, students as well as faculty members, including some of the leading minds of the university. We had a long and exciting discussion. I learned it is possible to have a genuine conversation with Israelis on the subject of Jewish religion, provided it takes place in an atmosphere in which people feel free to express themselves without fear that what they say may be used for partisan purposes.

We do not sponsor religious services at the Hillel Foundation in Jerusalem. Jerusalem has no need for an additional synagogue. But there is a need for Jewish students to think objectively about Jewish religion, not in terms of the tensions between state and religion that exist in Israel, but in terms of an approach that views religion as the great tradition of the Jewish people—a tradition which merits consideration first in objective, academic terms, then as an aspect in the life of the community, and ultimately as an aspect of one's personal existence. In this sense, religion is basic to the work of Hillel Foundations wherever they may be located.

Let me describe another facet of our program. Just before I left, fifty Arab students met at *Beit Hillel.* When they first told me they would like to meet in Hillel House, I had the feeling that even in Israel, Hillel was called upon to conduct some kind of "interfaith program." The group had been meeting in the YMCA, under auspices not always friendly to Israel. I felt it would help them and us to have them meet in Hillel House and to extend to them the same kind of hospitality which Christian associations have frequently extended to us in American universities.

They invited me to open their first meeting with a few words of welcome. Since I did not want to talk about group relations or to touch political issues, I decided to speak about Hillel the Elder. Speaking in Hebrew, I told something about his life, thought, and conception of human conduct: "Do not do unto others what is hateful unto you." When the chairman rose to thank me—he spoke in Hebrew, too—he said, "What a wonderful slogan for this country! Is it really impossible for us to live in this spirit?"

If you wish, this is an interfaith program too. It is different from the interfaith activities we find in the United States. Yet it is based on the same recognition that human beings must learn to live together in fellowship.

But Hillel's most important function, as I see it, is probably reflected in an incident involving one of the young leaders of an extreme Orthodox group [Meah Sh'arim] that is opposed to the Jewish state.

We had planned a series of lectures on Franz Rosenzweig, the distinguished German-Jewish thinker, in commemoration of the twenty-fifth anniversary of his death. The lecturers included Professors Hugo Bergmann, Ernst Simon, Jacob Fleishman, and Nathan Rotenstreich.

Martin Buber was in the audience and after one of the lectures I saw him talking to a young man who wore the traditional *caftan* and skull cap. Professor Buber introduced us but I did not catch the young man's name. He told me that he had enjoyed the program and that, even though he did not agree with everything that had been said, he was delighted that Franz Rosenzweig was being discussed in Jerusalem. Could he come over and talk to me sometime?

The following morning a friend telephoned and told me that the young man was Leibele Weisfish from Meah Sh'arim.[1] Meah Sh'arim, far away—not geographically but culturally and religiously—had come to Rechaviah where Hillel is located to listen quietly to a lecture on Franz Rosenzweig. I did not think Mr. Weisfish would come back, but he did. He wanted information on the Hillel Foundation. It was surprising to see how a man, belonging to a group that is usually pictured as extremist and intolerant of other peoples' views, could be deeply appreciative of what we were trying to do. He knew I was not of his persuasion. He knew the Hillel Foundation was open to all students—Western, Eastern, believers as well as nonbelievers. He wondered whether our approach would "bring the students closer to God," but added, "Obviously you have got to do it this way." And he went so far as to suggest that Hillel could make a

1. Literally, "hundred-fold" (Genesis 26:12) or "hundred gates." Name of a quarter of Jerusalem established in 1875 and protected by a wall with many gates. Center of settlement of religious Orthodoxy in Jerusalem.

significant contribution to Israel's life by arranging a translation of Rosenzweig into Hebrew.

This kind of experience, isolated though it may be, is nevertheless a good example of what a Hillel Foundation can be. It points to what I am convinced is our greatest task—building a common ground for all convictions and developing a sense of community among those who are often profoundly divided.

I know it will take a long time for the different groups to develop a sense of community and discover the possibilities of fellowship, interaction and intercommunication for which we are striving and which we have achieved in the United States (at least to a certain degree). Yet more and more students and young people in Israel are beginning to sense the importance of this concept. To nurture its growth is probably one of the most significant contributions which the Hillel Foundation can make, not only in Israel, but wherever we are called upon to serve.

Excerpts from letters and
reports from Israel,
1950-1955.

ON ISRAEL AND AMERICAN JEWRY

The first house in which our family lived after our arrival in Jerusalem was on Ramban Street, our second domicile was on Rashba, the third on Arlozoroff Street. And in the neighborhood were streets and avenues named Maimonides, Ruppin, Ibn Shapruth, Ibn Gabirol, Keren Kayemet, King George. I mention this to indicate something of the geographic and cultural atmosphere of life in Israel. There, Jewish history is not the topic of a Sunday school lesson or university lecture—it is all around you. When you look out upon the mountains of Judea you are not just remembering, but experiencing a past become present.

In Israel, past and present seem to merge into a fullness and naturalness of Jewish living unequalled anywhere else. And you scarcely notice that beneath this naturalness there are tensions and clashes of historic and contemporary movements and ideas of Jews of different tribes and civilizations, struggling to give form and definition to the evolving life of this nation.

Years ago, when I was lecturing on the problems of Jewish persons in our time, I used to say that a Jewish homeland would help give Jews clarity of definition. The central psychological problem of many young Jews, as I saw it, lay in their inability to define themselves clearly and adequately. Their frequent discussions on "What are the Jews—race, nation, nationality, religious community?" were part of a fundamental personal quest for an answer to a deeply felt question: Who am I? This persistent questioning and self-questioning was ultimately related to the problems of Jewish collective self-definition in the modern world. Lacking the fullness of a real definition that was derived from the whole-ness and adequacy of their experience as Jews, they sought a verbal construction that would help them explain their name and fate.

I felt that a North Dakota farmer, for instance, may not be able to define an American any more clearly than you can define a Jew. But the North Dakota farmer has neither the need for, nor the urge toward verbal self-definition. The things he does and the way he does them are sufficient to explain to himself and his neighbors who and what he is. Similarly, your grandfather and mine found little need for engaging in Jewish definition-making. In just a few words they could explain adequately who they were and why. The situation of their grandchildren is quite different. A Jewish homeland, I used to conclude, would give Jews in the modern world a clarity of definition that had its roots in the whole-ness of human life as experienced and expressed by the Jewish people living in its historic homeland.

The establishment of Israel has not produced this clarity of definition. It has created the Israeli, the citizen of a new state. But the question of the relationship between *Israeli* and *Jew* continues to occupy the minds of thoughtful persons in Israel.

Implied in this question are a number of additional questions. What is the historic link between the present state of Israel and the religious and cultural tradition of the Jewish people? What is the relationship between the Jews in Israel and those of other lands? What should be their relationship, if any? Those who, like the Canaanites, wish to free themselves from the "burdens" of the Jewish past beginning with the ghetto and going back to Father Abraham, deny also the desirability of a relationship with Jews outside Israel. They constitute only a tiny minority, and we need not consider them here, although their ideas may be more important than some people think. For most Jews in Israel, whatever their party affiliation, be it religious or secular, the establishment of the state is the clearest affirmation of a historic continuity and link with the cultural—if not religious—traditions of the Jewish people. The precise meaning of this link with the past and its role in contemporary life is far from clear. Israelis are still too much absorbed in the daily problems of economic and political instability, too much under the impact of the miraculous reconstruction of the state, to give serious thought to this problem.

They do have a strong sense of kinship with Jews elsewhere. Their desire for continued relationship with them—especially with the Jews of the United States—is beyond question. But their view of the position and the future of the American Jewish community inevitably affects the terms and quality of the relationship. This view, no matter how phrased, comes generally close to the Zionist theory of *shelilath hagolah* [negation of diaspora].

According to this theory, Jewish life in the diaspora is in a process of disintegration that cannot be reversed. Since the breakdown of the ghetto we have witnessed the disintegration of the Jewish community structure, the Jewish educational pattern, and the organic character of Jewish life characteristic of the ghetto. The corrosive forces of assimilation and anti-Semitism have undermined the foundations of the way of life peculiar to the ghetto. And the religion which gave meaning and sanction to that way of life has lost its potency. Jews remain Jewish—or survive—in the diaspora largely because they are forced to. Their Jewishness becomes a verbal kind of religion and results in a narrowed concept of historic Judaism on the one hand and in shabbiness and self-hatred on the other. Imposed or voluntary segregation, at times geographic—more often social and cultural—constitutes the condition of Jewish survival in the diaspora. Only in Israel can Jews regain the wholeness of human experience, i.e., share in the cultural and spiritual treasures of the world and remain Jewish at the same time.

This theory makes no distinction between the different *golahs* and assumes a similar fate ultimately for all Jewries outside Israel.

At its best, the prevalent Israeli attitude toward American Jews engenders both a genuine concern for their fate and a desire to save them. Along with this goes an almost unavoidable deprecation of the American Jews' presumably misguided and futile efforts—political or religious—at saving themselves. At its worst, this tends to support and encourage a disdain for what they consider to be the rich but second-rate Jews of the American *golah*.

In any case, this attitude is bound to postpone the development of a sound basis for fruitful interplay between Israel and the American Jewish community. It tends to limit their relationship to exhortations to philanthropy, often moving and generous, frequently vulgar and not enough.

As yet, little has been done to develop new patterns of relationship. Few Israelis can conceive of American Jews contributing in other than material or political ways. In the light of their analysis of the present and future of the American Jewish community, they can hardly envision that it will share creatively, either now or in the future, in a renascent Jewish cultural and spiritual enterprise. With the impact of their heroism and accomplishments in war and in peace still strong, they see themselves as the sole guardians of the Jewish heritage, its hopes and its strength.

The Americans "educated" by Israelis to believe that

there is no salvation "in absentia" and that the only real relation with Israel is immigration to it, are forced into increased
self-reliance. Although the Israelis have failed, for the time
being at least, to persuade Americans to accept their analysis
of the Jewish position in America, they seem to have had
considerable success in prompting many Americans to relin-
quish their long-cherished faith in the preservative and creative influences of the reborn Jewish homeland upon their
own cultural and spiritual life.

If in spite of this, interest in Israel—aside from historic
attachment and philanthropy—still continues strong in many
places in the United States, it is due largely to a stubborn
belief that a mutually productive cultural and spiritual relationship is absolutely essential for the preservation of the
Jewish heritage in the modern world.

There is reason to believe that such a relationship might yet
evolve. More and more people are inquiring: What is the
meaning of the state? What is it to become? What is to be
the nature of the link between the Israel of today and the
Israel of history? Isolated today, and probably forever a
minority in the Arab world, Israel will need both deep roots
in the Jewish past and close links with the Jewries outside
of Israel to maintain its spiritual and cultural identity among
the nations.

To sensitive and thoughtful people in Israel, the clarity of
geographic and political boundary lines will only sharpen the
questions of historic relationship and spiritual definition, of
religious meanings and values, in the new state.

In their search for deep roots in the Jewish past, Israelis
will come upon many of the fundamental problems of spiritual readjustment and re-evaluation of various aspects of
Jewish tradition which Jews in other lands have faced and
are facing. How can we make the past insights, commandments, and moral visions relevant and applicable to our own
times, to our own lives? How can we become properly

attuned to the voices of God and prophet in this new age? These are questions not peculiar to any place. Despite the vast difference between Jewish life in Israel and the *golah*, and despite the peculiar urgencies, motives, and weight that their respective situations assign to these questions, there is a core for a common quest.

The answers to the questions, and the search for them, form part of the task of spiritual self-definition in which Jews in Israel will sooner or later have to engage. In this task, which is beyond geography and politics, there is need and place for common effort. We shall have to keep together spiritually in order not to be lost in the world.

This common effort on the part of Jews in Israel and the United States will call for a new orientation and a new concept of relationships based on the following presuppositions:

Jews in Israel and Jews in the *golah* stand in a dynamic relationship of equal but different parts of one whole.

The *whole* is the world-wide Jewish community known historically as the Jewish people which includes today, as it always has, the Jews of *Eretz Israel* and those of other lands.

By *equal but different*, I have in mind what Horace Kallen terms the "parity of the different" in the give-and-take of democratic interplay. This implies equal rights, duties, and opportunities to express the different functions (and potential functions) peculiar to each part of the whole.

Each part may be dominant or recessive (or dominant in certain spheres of activity and recessive in others at one and the same time) depending upon its potency, stage of development, historic situation, and needs of the other parts.

The interaction of the different parts of the whole, or to use Professor Kallen's term—their "orchestration"—constitutes the dynamic relationship between Israel and the rest of world Jewry.

For this re-orientation to come about we shall require the

will to believe that it *can* come about. And we shall have to work toward it and create instruments of personal and institutional intercommunication that will explain us more adequately to Israel and Israel to us. Above all, we in the United States shall have to deepen our faith and our knowledge of the historic tradition which is the common source of our being. We shall have to make the faith of our fathers our faith, a faith to live by that will give direction and purpose to our thoughts and acts as Jews, as human beings.

Thus strengthened by knowledge and commitment, we shall be able to discover a common language with those in Israel and elsewhere who are concerned with maintaining and expressing the uniqueness of our tradition in our time. From our different perspectives—the Israelis as members of a Jewish nation in its own homeland in the East, and we as members of a cultural and religious minority in the American democracy in the West—we shall each contribute the uniqueness of our vision and effort to our common cultural and spiritual enterprise.

Excerpts from address,
National Hillel Summer
Institute, Camp High Point,
near Kingston, New York,
August 27, 1953.

I speak to you on this subject not as an expert—I lived too long in Israel to be able to qualify as such. But during my five-year stay in Israel I had the opportunity of observing and sharing in the life and thought of Israelis, especially of students, teachers, and writers. I had occasion to be with them in their homes; sit with them in their cafés; speak to them and with them; listen to their conversations, arguments, and debates; share in their celebrations of holidays and festivals; hear and overhear their remarks about those who are like them and unlike them—Israelis and Americans— and gather some impressions and perhaps some insights into their thoughts concerning themselves and others.

In this paper I shall not concern myself with the political aspects of Jewish religion in Israel, the conflicting views concerning Sabbath observance, *kashrut* [dietary practices], marriage, and "church" and state. I shall limit myself to a discussion of the psychological and intellectual setting within which these problems arise and have their being.

The problem of religion is not of course a problem peculiar to Israel. It is the problem of Western man and the problem of Jews wherever they are. I shall speak primarily of some of the Jewish aspects of the problem, specifically the Israeli ones.

One day during my first year in Jerusalem the daughter of a professor at the Hebrew University dropped in to see us. She was a high school senior whose parents had come to Israel with the second *aliyah*.[1] Ariella found me reading some Hebrew poetry. On the table was a book of poems by a contemporary Israeli poet. "How do you like him?" she asked. "Oh," I said, "He is a good poet but there are many like him in the literature of the world." She looked at the volume in my hand, a collection of poems by Yosef Tsvi Rimon. "What about him?" I told her that Rimon impressed me very much. "He is in the great tradition of Jewish religious poetry," I added. "No wonder you like him," she remarked, *"hu kol kach galuti"* (he is so full of exile mentality).

Galut and *galuti*—these are key words, although not the only ones, for our understanding of the sabra [native-born Israeli] mentality and of the attitudes of many young Israelis to the Jewish past and to Jewish religion. What is the meaning of these words? I can, perhaps, explain them best by referring to the monologue of Yudke, the hero of Hazaz' story, *Ha-d'rashah* (The Sermon).

> I want to announce (says Yudke at the kibbutz meeting) . . . I want to announce that I am opposed to the history of the Jews. . . . We are a people without a history. We are not the makers of history. . . . It's the *goyim* who made it. Just as they put out our lights on the Shabbat and milked our cows on the Shabbat and fired our furnaces, so too they made our history. That's why I am opposed to it. That's why it does not exist for me. *Eyni m'kabel otah!* Not one line of it, not one jot. Nothing.

1. Second wave of immigration to Israel.

Just think about it. What is there in it? Accusations, libels, oppression, *kiddush ha'shem*.[2] And again and again the same thing, endlessly. Boring to death . . . simply boring.

Of course there is strength in the capacity to withstand all the edicts and tribulations. But that's the kind of strength I don't like. First of all, I should like you to understand me, this is *gvurah b'ley breyrah*—it's courage without choice. Courage without alternatives is not courage . . . you are forced into it. Secondly, in the course of time this strength, this capacity for suffering becomes a great weakness, a special capacity for the hideous and the shameful . . . and a love for it. . . . Suffering keeps us alive. . . . Without it we cannot live. . . . Have you ever seen a community of Jews without suffering? I, never. A Jew who is not suffering is a strange creature . . . almost not a Jew at all . . . *chatzi goy* [half a non-Jew] . . . In a certain sense, ugliness and shame, the capacity to suffer it, is also strength and courage. We are precisely that kind of people. We are not fighters, we are not conquerors, we are not rulers. On the contrary, we are the conquered, suffering endlessly, willingly and with love. . . . With a kind of nocturnal psychology, we have managed to devise a tremendous structure of the mind to enable us to go through life as the subjugated and persecuted, and to find uniqueness in our fate. The most audacious and fantastic construct we have resorted to is a

2. "Sanctification of the divine name." The term originally connoted only martyrdom, but it was later extended to apply also to all acts of strict observance and integrity which reflected creditably upon Judaism and the Jewish people.

vicious triad, known as *galut, kiddush ha'shem,* and
mashiach [Messiah].

. . . *Galut, galut.* Oh, how they love it, and how
they hold on to it. So holy, so beloved, intimate,
familiar; so close to the heart . . . nearer than Jerusalem, more Jewish than Jerusalem, more deeply
rooted, more spiritual . . . *galut* is our pyramid.
Its base is *kiddush ha'shem* and its apex, *mashiach.*

One thing is perfectly clear . . . Zionism is not
continuity with the Jewish past . . . not a continuation of Jewish history, but the contrary. It
is the opposite of that which was . . . it is the
end of it. Not renewal but beginning. And he who
does not think so is only fooling himself. Indeed
eretz yisrael zeh k'var lo yahadut! [3] This is already
true, and will be especially so in the future. . . .

The story of Yudke is important, not because everything
he says accurately mirrors the spirit of Israel today, but
because his image of *galut—galut* and the religion of *galut—*
is shared, to a significant degree, consciously or subcon-
sciously, by many in Israel today.

If you will stop to reflect upon this, you will realize that
Yudke's image of *galut* and of the religion of the ghetto is
not peculiar to him and his sabra compatriots. It has hovered
over much of Jewish thought and experience in the modern
world. What, in some ways at least, is Reform Judaism or
Conservative Judaism? What are most Jewish movements in
the last one hundred years if not attempts at rejection of
galut and ghetto? The ghost of the ghetto and the problems
of ghetto and emancipation are still with us as psychological
fact, as historic memory and inheritance, as unreleased tension. And for two hundred years now the shadow of ghetto,

3. The land of Israel already is no longer [identical with] Judaism.

the memory of suffering, and the fear of its repetition have led many Jews to extremes in their efforts at dissociation.

The spiritual heirs of Yudke in organized form were the Canaanites—a sort of nativist Israeli group founded, ironically enough but perhaps naturally, by an immigrant. They, like Yudke, were tired of Jewish history, of the burdens of the Jewish past, its divine claims, its messianic visions. They considered themselves Hebrews rather than Jews. The history of the Jews between the loss of the Hebrew state and its re-establishment eight years ago was not their history.

The Canaanites have almost disappeared. Their official organ, *Aleph*, is no longer being published. But their ideas and the mentality which they reflect cannot be disregarded entirely. The disdain of ghetto and *galut* and of a religion reminiscent of ghetto and *galut* is not limited to them. In a real sense there is a Canaanite lurking in the mind and heart of many an Israeli. But may I add, parenthetically, what I have already implied earlier: there is at least a fraction of one per cent (and perhaps more!) of a Canaanite hidden in almost every emancipated Jew in the Western world. But it has become fashionable to slur over the Canaanite within us, lost as we are in computation of the statistical growth of Jewish religion in this country. It was not so long ago that we too were rejecting the religion our fathers brought with them to this land. A generation or two ago, and I dare say even today, many of us were (or still are) exceedingly sensitive to the *galut* image and ghetto accent of Jewish religion. I don't think I need document this statement.

Beneath the naturalness of Jewish living in Israel one cannot help but sense the tensions and clashes of historic and contemporary world views as the new nation struggles to give form and definition to its evolving life. Today the religion of *galut* and ghetto and the secularism of our age are face-to-face in a dramatic and fateful encounter in the new setting of the state of Israel. Neither state nor synagogue has worked out the new meaning and role of Jewish religion in the life of a Jewish state. Each makes claims upon the other: secularism, in the name of democratic nationalism; religion, in the name of divinely ordained commandments to which many Jews in Israel, as elsewhere, no longer respond.

But with all their rejection of ghetto and *galut*, for the great majority of Jews in Israel, the establishment of the state is the clearest affirmation of Jewish continuity and link with the cultural—if not the religious—traditions of the Jewish people. The word they like to use in describing that link with the past is *massoret* rather than *dat*. The precise meaning of that term is not always clear (any more than is our use of the term *tradition*), but we shall not be far wrong if we say that *massoret* refers to tradition without God or with a very hazy God, while *dat*, or religion, refers to tradition inseparable from God—Torah and *mitzvot*. In any case, this kind of link with the Jewish past, through *massoret* rather than *dat*, is again not peculiar to Israelis. (I dare say there are many Jews in the United States, including some presidents of synagogues and temples, who are *massoret*-minded.) But what is the nature of this link with the past? What does the word "Jewish" mean?

I recall that shortly after our arrival in Israel, my wife and I were invited to the Artists' Chanukkah Ball in Jerusalem. The Artists House, near the King David Hotel, was festively decorated. The decorative designs created by the artists were ingenious and colorful. And in the dimly-lit hall hundreds of couples danced to the lively rhythms of American and South American dance music or chatted with their friends. It was an exciting and bustling affair. From the appeals of agencies which raise funds for Israel one would never guess how pleasant and delightful life in Israel can be. But where was Chanukkah? I wondered. On the way out, our hosts asked,

"Well, how did you like it?" "It was very delightful," I said, "but frankly we expected something else, something different. Tell us, where was *Chanukkah?*" Their answer was clear: "Stop looking for *dos pintele yid*" (the Jewish angle of things, or as we might put it, for Jewish content). "Here everything is Jewish." But I continued asking myself: What *is* Jewish?

As I continued living in Israel, getting to know its people, reading its newspapers and journals, listening to discussions and debates, I realized I was not the only one trying to discover the meaning of the word *Jewish*. About four years ago Professor Ernst Simon published his provocative article, *"Ha'im od yehudim anachnu?"*("Are We Still Jews?"). The Jerusalem Writers' Association considered the statement sufficiently important and controversial to arrange for a highbrow discussion of it. Unhappily, the discussion was far from highbrow. The confusion of categories—national (or ethnic) and religious—that characterizes so much of our discussion of Jewish religion in the United States was repeated there. But the discussion did generate enough heat to suggest the liveliness of the topic. And although there seemed to be much evasion of the issue, it was quite clear that the question of relationship between *Jew* and *Israeli* was of fundamental concern to a considerable number of thoughtful people.

During my stay in Israel, especially during the last three years, numerous articles on this subject appeared in newspapers and magazines. I am referring to the secular press and periodical literature in particular—this question is naturally a major preoccupation of the religious press. [The Israeli newspapers] *Ha'aretz* and *Davar*, *Mevo'ot* and *Molad*, *Gil'yonot* and *B'terem* have again and again published earnest and often penetrating discussions, written by the younger writers as well as those of the older generation. In them and in the lively correspondence to the editors which they stimulated, you discover that the concern with Jewish religion in Israel has two major aspects: first, it centers about the problem of historic continuity and the nature of the unity of Israelis and the Jews of the diaspora; second, it grows out of personal need— a yearning and a groping for the meaning of life. In this paper I am concerned with the second aspect.

Some time ago at a conference devoted to the relation between Israel and the diaspora, S. Yizhar, one of the very able young writers and a Mapai representative in the Knesset, raised the question: *ba'meh ani yehudi* and *ba'meh ani yisraeli?* [4] The latter he could answer with ease; the former was more difficult. There is no need going into his reasons at this time. What I am interested in pointing out is this: the confusion of categories—the national and the religious—is beginning to give way to an awareness of the religious dimension in Israeli life. "Here everything is Jewish" (i.e., the experience of majority status, the identification of all that Jews do as Jewish, the language and the landscape), is no longer adequate. *"Ba'meh ani yehudi?"* is beginning to assert itself, and with it is developing a critical examination of both terms—*yisraeli* and *yehudi*—and their relationship, their claims upon each other. The question of Jewish religion as historic claim upon this generation and future generations of Israelis, as a group and as individuals, is earnestly and insistently addressing itself to a small but growing number of thoughtful persons in Israel.

The concern with religion in a personal sense is closely related, among other things, to postwar disillusionment and waning idealism in the younger generation. While the religious or nonreligious attitudes of sabras are not new to this generation, the lack of idealism is. Their fathers and mothers were for the most part nonreligious, and in some instances even anti-religious. But they had religious roots—they were the *yeshiva bachurim* [5] from the ghettos of Russia and Poland who transmuted their religious yearnings into movements of

4. "Wherein am I a Jew and wherein am I an Israeli?"
5. Students at a talmudic academy.

social justice, visions of a new society, and saw in their work
and in their life a *dat ha'avodah* [religion of labor].

A perceptive young Israeli poet, Yitzhak Shalev, suggests
the difference between the generations in terms of *hasidim*
and *mitnagdim* [6]:

> Those of the present generation are apt to sing
> and dance as did the earlier ones, and perhaps even
> more. But their *hora* [7] never reaches the heights of
> Hasidic ecstasy through which the earlier genera-
> tion found religious expression—the generation that
> departed from its religion but retained the deep
> yearnings of the religious spirit. . . . For the *hora* is
> not the appropriate dance for the secular spirit
> which is better trained for the swayings of social
> recreation than for the ritual circle (of the *hora*).
> . . . This is the generation of the *mitnagdim*—the
> rationalists. Now that the war has been won, the
> state established, the young are without an ideal to
> claim their lives; amidst a drab and visionless exist-
> ence they have fallen prey to "Americanizatzia,"
> the dominant secularism of the world [best sym-
> bolized for Shalev by Hollywood]. . . . The absence
> of a spirit of religiosity, on the one hand, and reli-
> gious content on the other, robs this generation
> of the spiritual resources that would protect them
> in their mighty encounter with the secularism of
> this world and makes them easy targets for its
> crassness and materialism. . . .

In this situation that has come about since the

6. "Opponents." The opponents of the Hasidic movement, so-called
after the issuance of a religious ban against the Hasidim by the Gaon
of Vilna in 1772.
7. Israeli folk dance.

establishment of the state there remained only one
hope for a decisive change: a new rapprochement
between our youth and Jewish religion. But here
occurred one of the most frightful things in our
history. The greatest tragedy of Judaism in our
time I see in the fact that it has not succeeded in
finding a way to the heart of Israeli youth; and
the tragedy of our youth is that it has not succeeded in being accessible to it. The cause of it I
find not only in those responsible for the education
of our youth, beginning with the first *aliyot*, nor in
the general secularism of the world, but first and
foremost in the representatives of formal Judaism
in Israel. These men stubbornly refused to understand that the coming together of our youth and
Judaism is imperative for the survival of both; and
they so represented Judaism that the spirit of our
youth would abhor it. It was clear from the very
beginning that the sabra would not come close to
a type of Judaism that is intent upon perpetuating
the *galut* mentality in the forms of *meah shearim*.
. . . This means that the greatest catastrophe of
Judaism arises from those who represent it.

In these discussions of religion and the searchings and
gropings of youth in Israel, you often hear references to
Jewish religion as it has developed in the United States and
elsewhere, as it has adjusted itself to the needs of modern
man. The "adjustment" of religion is something many Israelis
cannot understand. I am not referring to the attitude of those
committed to historic Orthodox religion. I have in mind
particularly those who have difficulty in accepting Orthodox
religion as practiced in Israel. They cannot believe in that
religion, neither can they understand adaptations of it. "Those

who call for the adjustment of Jewish tradition to the demands of our generation," says Boaz Evron, writing in *Ha'aretz* of November 11, 1955, "do not know what they are talking about, and they are, in effect, testifying to a deprecation and lack of understanding of Judaism." He continues:

> They seem to think that Judaism is a kind of cloth that the tailor can cut to measure, in accordance with his "modern taste." Religions are not for sale. . . . In religion there are no "values" that can be taken out of their organic context and made to harmonize with our taste. . . .

Thoughtful Israelis cannot quite understand the looseness of definition implied in our [American] use of the term *religion*, where religion has often come to be a synonym for moral conduct, charitable activity, attendance at religious services on Yom Kippur or membership in a synagogue. They look suspiciously upon our definition of ourselves as a religious community. What passes for religion among us—the activities of our sisterhoods and men's clubs, the Jewish education of our children, the sermons and lectures of our rabbis, the projects of our community or synagogue centers—all these, as they see them, are dominantly expressions of ethnic life. Religion for us, they believe, is in most instances but a convenient word for group identity, an expedient term defining our desire for ethnic continuity in a setting where religious pluralism is looked upon more favorably than cultural pluralism. Religious nostalgia and perhaps even commitments form part of it, but these are not central to our personal or group identity as Jews. (And is it not true that much of American Jewish religion for the last twenty, thirty years has been a kind of "gimmick" in the service of "survival"— Jew-consciousness rather than God-consciousness?)

For the Israeli, religion—as an object of assent or dissent—is too important a word to be used lightly. In a country where ideologies have shaped the lives and thoughts of many people, where party identity has for many years determined one's mode of life and action, words, platforms, and systems of thought are examined critically by thoughtful people. It is not just a constellation of activities that man lives by. His activities are related to systems of thought or ideologies that give direction and meaning to them. This applies even more to religion. Again I refer to Evron:

> The prophets of the return to religion do not even understand what becoming religious means. It would seem that they picture the return as the lighting of Sabbath candles, going to synagogue to enjoy *kol nidrei*.[8] This is not return to religion.

As Evron and others have indicated, the answer to the problem of Jewish religion in Israel lies not—at least for the serious and thoughtfully searching Jewish intellectuals—in what Evron terms *chatzi dat* [half-religion], a lessening of the burden. What they are searching for, now that many of them have lost faith in party ideology and political panaceas, is a faith, an ideal that is capable of claiming their total life, their whole loyalty—not a lesser claim than the party had upon them but at least as great a claim upon their thought and act and sentiment.

Under these circumstances the road to religious identity and religious commitment is hard and full of obstacles. Neither in act nor in thought does Orthodox Jewish religion in Israel speak to the mind and heart of the young people. To quote Boaz Evron again:

8. Prayer intoned at the beginning of the worship service ushering in the Day of Atonement.

Judaism will have to undergo a prophetic revival to
be able to inspire those of our generation. Such a
catastrophic or revolutionary revival would, in
effect, mean a new religion, such as the revolution
that gave birth to Christianity. . . . Religion is too
powerful and elemental a force to be contained
within the hazy, convenient modern framework of
"values" . . . that lukewarm soup is not the substance out of which religious revivals arise. And
that nostalgia for tradition that has become so popular in certain circles in our land is but cheap sentimentality that shames both the religion and the
nostalgic sentimentalists. The pious Jew is fully
justified in looking disdainfully upon them. The
meah shearim Jew will die *al kiddush ha'shem* but
not the Reform one nor the sentimentalist. And I
know of no better test of the earnestness of one's
religious *kavanah* [inner devotion].

Evron and others like him can understand and in some ways
even admire the *meah shearim* Jew and Orthodox Jewish
religion. But they cannot accept them. Religion, like the ideologies of our time, must have a systematic explanation, a metaphysical basis acceptable to the "modern" mind.

In the metaphysical realm, Judaism is grappling
with the same problems that other great religions
have grappled with and not found a solution for.
And where is the difference between the religious
section of Israeli Jewry and its nonreligious group?
. . . The difference is in demands for Sabbath observance and prohibition of *chazir* [pork] and the
like—demands that have no ethical meaning. . . .
There is not even one political-ethical question since

the establishment of the state that has called forth a
vigorous ethical response from the religious section
of Israeli Jews, a response that is not ambiguous.
Perhaps these Jews do not represent the deeper
implications of Judaism. . . . But the only ways we
can judge the spiritual and ethical qualities of religion is by the acts and the vitality of its adherents.
Thus judged, we must arrive at the only possible
conclusion, namely that Jewish religion has ceased
being a vital force, fruitful and fructifying. . . .
And yet we shall be doing violence to the truth,
if we maintain that *ha'maor she'ba'yahadut* [9] is
only a rhetorical phrase. . . . Jewish tradition con-
tains a mighty ethical structure which, thanks to
the precision with which it determined every detail
of man's life, from birth to death, has succeeded in
giving a decisive spiritual image to many generations. But there comes a time when a tradition is
no longer susceptible to change and readjustment.

So much is being written and spoken about Jewish religion
in Israel that some people have come to see signs of the
beginning of a religious revival there. All kinds of reasons
are being given for the need to return to religion. In response
to these, Amitai Etzioni wrote a vigorous attack entitled
"*Tzvi'ut lo to'il*" ["Hypocrisy will not help"]. "No," he says,
"we are still far from a religious revival." Above all, he main-
tains, these hypocritical exhortations to a return to religion
on pedagogic grounds—religion as mental hygiene, as escape
from the horrors of the atomic age—will find little response
in the hearts of young Israelis. That's not the religion they
are looking for, and "The traditional way to God is shut
before us."

9. "The radiance [light, luminousness] that is Judaism.

There is, indeed, Etzioni continues, a kind of ferment in our midst . . . we are disillusioned, and are groping and searching. Perhaps we had expected too much from the establishment of the state . . . perhaps what's happened to us was inevitable. . . .

> This disillusionment has led some of my friends to careerism, to the pursuit of the pleasures of the moment. Of those I am not speaking here. I am concerned with those for whom this disillusionment has caused pain and problems demanding a solution, a pain too acute to live with in peace, to resign oneself to. It gives us no peace. . . . We search for an answer. In our search we encounter traditional Judaism and the *Tanakh*.[10] They demand of us a relationship. But there is an awareness growing within us that we do not know them. They have been presented to us in a distorted way: the Bible as a collection of quotations in approval of Zionism and tree-planting on Tu B'shvat,[11] and Judaism as a conflict between *ya'lag*[12] and the rabbis, boring couplets of medieval poetry. . . . We are striving to overcome the wall between us. . . . We are trying to come to a new understanding of the Jews of the *golah* and of the *Tanakh*, an understanding that would help to provide us with a setting and basis for a new evaluation. . . . But, *al ta'itzu banu* . . . do not rush us, please. If we are

10. Hebrew Bible, from the initial letters *Torah* (Pentateuch), *Nevi'im* (Prophets), *Ketubim* (Hagiographia).

11. Fifteenth day of the Hebrew month of Shevat. The date marks the dividing line for fruit tithing. Observed as Arbor Day (New Year of Trees).

12. Initials of Judah Loeb Gordon, leading Hebrew poet of the Russian *Haskalah* (enlightenment), b. Vilna 1830, d. St. Petersburg 1892.

to return we must do it ourselves, directed by our experiences, and no one else can direct us. *Al ta'itzu banu.*

I have quoted at length from Israeli writers—most of them young men—to indicate both the claim that Jewish religion seems to have upon them as well as their difficulties in responding to that claim. Attracted and repelled, wanting to believe but incapable, they find little help in their search from those who officially speak for Jewish religion in Israel.

In any case it is clear, I believe, that their predicaments are not peculiar to them. They are the predicaments of religion in our time. They are specifically the problems of Jewish religion in Israel, as well as everywhere else. The questions they raise about God and man, about faith and commandments, are questions that cannot be easily, glibly answered— and they are less easily answered in Israel than in the United States. The deeper the question, the more difficult the answer. And they are searching deeply, yearningly, and are less susceptible to fads than we are.

Their questions are ultimately our questions. And we must struggle together to find the answers. How can we make past insights, commandments and moral visions relevant and applicable to our own time, to our own lives? How can we become properly attuned to the voices of God and prophet in this world and in this time? What is the meaning of Torah and where is God? What is the meaning of Israel in Israel and outside it? And what is the relationship between past and present? These questions we have in common. With all our major reformations and minor adaptations of the Judaism of the *galut* and ghetto, we are no less in need of the answers for ourselves and our children than are the Israelis. For despite the vast difference between Jewish life in Israel and the United States, and the particular motives, urgencies, and weight that our respective situations assign to these questions, *we are ultimately in the same religious situation.*

Abridged version of an address delivered at Hebrew Union College–Jewish Institute of Religion, New York City, March 9, 1956, and at Convention of Rabbinical Assembly of America, Grossinger, New York, April 23, 1956.

Those who wish to liberate Judaism from what they call its ghetto mentality claim that the Jewish religion—or at least the Jewish religion as practiced in Israel—is merely an extension of ghetto mentality. It is *galut* imported into Israel. They oppose it vigorously. It must have no place in the new state. Moreover, there are many who are opposed to religion generally and who proclaim they came to Israel in order to break away from the past—in order to build a new land, a new people, and a new tradition. They want to begin from *aleph*. Actually almost every single Jew in the world has got something of this feeling within him— something of this rejection of the past, of the desire to start anew, of the wish to break away from those things which rise into consciousness when we use the terms *galut* or ghetto.

A great Hebrew novelist recently published a short story in which he describes the meeting of the Education Committee of his kibbutz. The members of the committee are trying to determine what to teach their children. In the midst of their discussion, a man who has contributed little to the discussion suddenly rises and says, "Don't define Zionism as a continuation of Jewish history. This is a lie, a betrayal of our hopes. Zionism does not aim to continue Jewish history. It aims to break with the past. We have had enough of martyrdom, of bookishness, of all those things which perpetuate the ghetto. We did not come here to continue this past. We came because we wanted to build something new—something which will grow out of our lives, something which is related to the sun and the stars and the soil and the trees and this land."

The novelist has eloquently caught our perennial desire to break with the past. In this respect, Israelis are not very different from American Jews, who also frequently feel they should break with the past, with martyrdom, the memories of the ghetto, and all that is associated with the term *galut*. Nevertheless, there is a significant difference between the rejection of the ghetto which you find in Israel and the rejection we find here. When the American Jew seeks to escape the past, he moves toward the image of the Christian world in which he lives. Israelis who reject the past do not necessarily want to become assimilated into the Christian world. They want to create something new. They look to a future which is Jewish at least in accordance with their definition of Jewishness. They look to an identity within their newly found freedom which will reflect their own strivings in a new land in which numerous permanent aspects of the Jewish past and of Jewish tradition continue to shape their identity.

For regardless of one's feelings about the Jewish past, one cannot live in Israel without being touched by it even while consciously rejecting it. The land is there still, as is the Bible. Both are part of the immediate experience of Israel's children. One cannot escape the Jewish past while wandering through Israel's landscape, speaking Hebrew, or reading the Bible. Whether one considers it holy or not, the past inevitably affects life and shapes it. Therefore there is reason to believe that despite the tensions and predicaments of Jews in Israel and despite their often understandable rejection of the past, the possibility exists that the Jewish life which will emerge in Israel will reflect both the past as well as the new experiences of Jews in their own land.

Excerpts from address,
National Hillel Summer
Institute, Camp B'nai B'rith,
Starlight, Pennsylvania,
August 30, 1954.

Aspects

Part 3

of Jewish Student Life

TO JEWISH STUDENTS

You have been described in a variety of ways. Teachers and all who have a deep concern with education and society have been quite curious about you. They have been writing books and articles about this generation, trying to discover what makes you tick. I have read that you are unexcitedly pleasure-seeking, skeptical, intellectually polite to your elders, but uninvolved in the intellectual struggle, that you have little sense or spirit of the intellectual adventure—you have no isms to argue about, to fight for or against. You are likely to be conformists, status seekers, organization men. For what is characteristic of this generation, we are told, is its acceptance of the values of its fathers. The conflicts of the generations—between parents and children—apparently do not take the form of rejection of parental values and of their notions of success and failure.

Like your parents you will be worshippers of many gods —respectable or not quite respectable gods—as are many educated and uneducated people in our times. They will be gods made in the market place or in the country club. They are man-made gods. Their home is within us. They are the ones who determine our actions, our estimate of ourselves, the things we aspire to, and the effort we expend on attaining them. But they derive their power over us not from our conviction of their truth or from the compelling power of a rationally achieved understanding. Their power over us— their mastery of our actions, the things we do or pretend we want to do, the clothes we wear, the books we read, and the movies we see—stems not from the *inner* man, but from the *other* man, the plurality of men, the group.

Universities, on a different plane and in a different way, are assemblages of little gods—departmental or interdepartmental gods. And while the professors may not claim godly prerogatives, man, being a worshipful creature, is as likely to worship the false gods as the true ones. The history of human thought and religion provides ample evidence.

For what we are all searching is something—be it a theory, a philosophy, or a religion—that will explain this confusing, frightening, and overwhelming world. The certainties of the past are no longer as certain as they used to be; the eternal verities are doubted; the tablets of the divine law—once the integrating factor in the lives of men, the source of coherent self-understanding and understanding of others—lie broken. We must pick up the pieces. We want more than pieces of knowledge, bits of information. We want something that will give our lives coherence and unity. We want help in discovering who we are and how to live, so that we may cease shifting from one position to another at the mercy of little gods and of conflicting values and loyalties that lay claim upon us.

*Excerpts from address to
Jewish students, B'nai B'rith
Hillel Foundation at the
University of Chicago,
undated.*

I̲t is now ten years since I began my work with Jewish students. I have lived with them, played with them, talked with them, listened to their confidential stories, their frivolous jests, their earnest protests, their self-questioning and their questioning of others, both men and God. All I know about them is based on what they have taught me—on my experience with them in thought and in fellowship. Through them I have seen historical forces become real in personal experience. I have seen the doubts, fears, illusions, and disillusionments of generations of Jews come to life in the day-by-day conduct of young people on American campuses. And I have observed the vague, remote happenings of the Jewish past dramatically re-enacted in the lives of freshmen, sophomores, juniors, and seniors from Rutland, Vermont; Kansas City; the Bronx; and Kalamazoo.

I say "dramatically" but not necessarily "conspicuously." Not that there are not conspicuous examples of Jewish group behavior on campus: the texture of the Jewish fraternity system, its mode of living, internal conflicts, the struggles between the Bronx and Park Avenue and pseudo-Park, their relationship to the YMCA and YWCA or their equivalents—all these have an accent related either directly or indirectly to the

Jewish name they bear. But on the whole, it is the inconspicuous, often unnoticed forms of Jewish behavior which
point to the nature of Jewishness in our time. The ordinary
observer, the nostalgic alumnus returning to "college town"
or fraternity row on the prewar campus might have difficulty
in discovering the predicaments of Jewish life on the campus.
The hilarity of drinking parties, the important positions occu-
pied by Jews on campus newspapers, the influence of the
Jewish BMOC (Big Man on Campus), the Jewish president
of the Young Women's Christian Association—all point to
Jewish well-being on campus. The Jewish football hero and
the Phi Beta Kappa men, the beautiful fraternity houses, the
sumptuously furnished sorority living rooms give little evidence that all is not well in Judaea.

But walk into the counselor's office on any campus in the
United States, talk to the Hillel director, or better still, win
your way into the intimate bull sessions in the fashionable
fraternities or the less fashionable campus "hangouts," and
you may get a glimpse of the dramatic but inconspicuous
fate of Jewish personality in the year 1944.

Last night I visited a Jewish fraternity. I was eager to chat
with the members of the house, eager to find out what they
were thinking about and to learn the effect of the cataclysmic
world changes upon their attitudes. I knew of course that
many of them would still be troubled by the fact of their
Jewishness. I realized that many were haunted by a feeling
of segregation. As long as the Christian world remains con-
stant in its attitude toward Jews, it is natural to expect a
degree of constancy in the attitudes of Jewish students towards
themselves and their neighbors. Still, I expected—perhaps
hoped for—some noticeable change in their attitude toward
themselves. The world was at war, and they themselves were
soon to fight it. They were seeing the fate of Jews headlined
in the newspapers. They had heard Jews and Judaism impli-
cated by friend and foe alike in the historic changes occurring

in the structure of man's life and thought. Surely they would reveal some change in their thinking about themselves and their fellow-Jews.

When they invited me to spend the evening with them I eagerly accepted. It was a day or two after the campus newspaper had announced the results of a student war bond rally. Without pre-arrangement the two Jewish fraternities and sororities—comprising two hundred out of the five thousand students at the university—subscribed more than twenty thousand dollars; the rest of the campus subscribed ten thousand dollars. I was curious as to the Jewish reaction regarding the unfriendly reception given the announcement in the paper. I was interested in hearing what they thought about their rival fraternity's decision not to accept publicly the trophy for the highest subscription to the war bond drive.

The house was alive with conversation about the bond drive, Jewish conspicuousness, and Christian-Jewish relations. Someone in the group pointed proudly to the YMCA trophy which was shining brightly on the mantlepiece. The fraternity had just won it for the second successive year for the largest contribution to the YMCA finance drive, and the proud young man considered it an example of Christian-Jewish cooperation. One of the pledges opened the house's scrapbook and showed me the story in the *Daily* about activities of the fraternity in connection with the drive. This is what I read:

FINANCE DRIVE RAISES $540.00
Phi Phi [Jewish Fraternity] subscribes largest amount for YMCA.

Results of the first day's activities of the YMCA student finance drive show that $540 of the $1200 pool has already been pledged, it was announced by Bernie Goldberg, Finance Chairman.

The individual with the highest amount of subscriptions received was Bernie Goldberg, while the leading team was team number three which is captained by Bernie Goldberg.

The fraternity which had subscribed the largest amount was Phi Phi. The fraternity or open house which subscribes the largest amount per man during the entire drive will receive the YMCA Finance Drive trophy, which last year was won by Phi Phi.

What did I think about it, he inquired. Did I think Jews should contribute to the YMCA? Of course they should, I replied. Organizations as liberal as the YMCA on our campus should have the support of everyone, including Jews. I referred specifically to the activities of the "Y" in behalf of the underprivileged on campus and of its struggle to have Negroes admitted to the dormitories of the university. Jews should support the "Y." But for the right reasons!

But what of the Jewish welfare fund? I asked. What of the needs of homeless Jewish refugees? I recalled to them the difficulties a student committee encountered in obtaining a contribution from their house for Jewish purposes. The discussion became heated. Referring to my comment that contributions to the "Y" should be properly motivated, a student in a Naval ROTC uniform reminded his fraternity brothers that the reasons the fraternity president gave for supporting the "Y" had little to do with the program of the "Y."

In the midst of the arguments, Sam Cohen, a senior, arose. He looked at me sharply. Then, slowly and deliberately, as if giving vent to long pent-up emotion, he spoke: "Judaism is not a religion." He paused for a moment. Heine's quip came to my mind. I thought he would quote the German Jewish poet in full: "It is a misfortune." But he did not. He stared at me rather resentfully and concluded: "It is obstinacy."

He was not quoting anybody. The thought he had expressed was original with him, born out of his experience and the experience of others like him. He was speaking for himself and for them, echoing the often shy and embarrassed and half-hidden thoughts and felings. "It is you, people like you," he continued vehemently, "who force it upon us, who perpetuate it. Why do you insist? Why do you keep reminding us of our Jewishness?" There was deep resentment in his voice, deep-felt hurt.

Sam Cohen was not speaking for all Jewish students. There are many who would repudiate his words. But there are many others—more than would care to admit it even to themselves—who share this resentment in varying degrees. In this resentment they find community—a sense of relationship with other Jews—an unconscious link with the precursors of their tribe in Israel.

* * *

Much has been written about the Jewish problem. Many have dealt with the horror and terror of Jews living in Nazi Europe. Too little attention has been given to the profound —although not as conspicuous—tragedy of Jewish personality in our time. In the discussions of the Jewish people and Jewish religion, the fate of the Jew in America—as humanbeing-born-Jew—has been submerged. Jewish periodicals speak of Jewish culture and tradition, of the disintegration of an ancient and hallowed heritage. But the fateful disintegration of Jewish persons—young and handsome American men and women—has been almost overlooked in the arguments and counterarguments for or against Zionism, for assimilation or survival. As if Jewish persons were only bricks in someone's imaginative edifice, not flesh and blood, frail mortal creatures in search of life, liberty, and the pursuit of happiness.

Like their fellow-students of Christian background, Jewish

students grope for meaning. They search for understanding of their position in this chaotic world. They try to develop a concept of life and to attain a sense of fellowship and at-homeness in the community to which they have come.

But wherever they turn, the ghost of their Jewishness, often a meaningless term, may turn up to bar their way. They may look for a room in one of the houses on campus and be told that Jews are not wanted. They may apply for a part-time job and be refused. They may listen to a classroom discussion and feel the argument was directed against them as Jews. They may write a paper and conclude the low grade was due to prejudice on the part of the professor. They may wish to make a date with a friend on campus and be refused. In all these instances, Jewishness may have nothing to do with their failure. But the world they live in assigns to it an evil quality, and they are especially sensitive to the evil meaning which the name carries.

For such is the potency of the name. It touches a person at scores of points during the day. One may be a Presbyterian, a Baptist, a Unitarian, or even a Catholic and not be consciously aware of that affiliation except at special times. But the sense of Jewishness persists. You meet a boy on campus. His name is Johnson. Yours is Frank. He seems to be friendly, and you wonder—what if he discovers you are Jewish? Should you tell him immediately? Perhaps it would be better to wait for an opportune moment. Perhaps. But should he discover your Jewishness before you tell him, he may think you were hiding it. So you tell him, and you drag it into the conversation by a reference to a synagogue which you have not attended for years, or to a Jewish magazine in the library that you would not ordinarily read. And then, on your way home, you wonder whether you did the right thing. Might he not have thought your reference to your Jewishness somewhat forced?

One day a Jewish boy, a brilliant student from a small

town in Ohio, dropped in to see me. In the course of the conversation, he expressed his disapproval of Jewish girls. He thought they were too showy, too interested in social status. "Who are your friends?" I inquired. "Gentiles," he said. "I date gentile girls." "Do they know you are Jewish?" "Well," he said hesitatingly, "they do. But I don't tell them immediately. I asked Jane for a date some time ago. We went out several times, and then after I was sure she liked me, I told her. You see if I had told her before she got to know me well, she might have refused to go out with me. Now that she has had a chance to get to know me, she learned that there were nice Jews in the world. In fact, you can see that this helps the Jewish people."

A humorous story, yet sad. It repeats itself in hundreds of instances and serves to underline the essential self-consciousness that Jewishness imposes upon Jews.

Jewishness is perhaps not the proper word. It is rather the designation *Jew*. With that name go a set of tangible or intangible problems which the student cannot entirely escape, no matter how insensitive he may be or what his particular experiences on campus may be.

As he begins to contemplate selection of a university, the question of his chances of admission to the school of his choice presents itself as a "Jewish" question. He may be conscious of his Jewish name. Perhaps there is a question on the application blank concerning his religious affiliation. As he stares at this question, all he has heard about quotas and discrimination converges upon him. And he interprets the question not as the university's innocent curiosity concerning religious affiliations of students, but rather as necessary information in determining his qualifications for admission. How shall he respond? Shall he admit his Jewishness and face the possibility of rejection? Shall he deny his convictions? He may feel the question is immoral and introduces an extraneous factor into the consideration of his eligibility. An immoral question might justify an immoral answer—a lie. This is the reasoning which some Jewish students will follow.

When the student comes to the campus, excited and hopeful, he cannot quite forget what he has heard or suspects about the university. Some of his friends were refused admission. They were better students, had higher scholastic averages than he. Why weren't they admitted? Was there a quota system? It could be, for he applied much later than they; yet he was admitted.

I need not examine the problem further. Every day may bring new questions, new problems. The effects of Jewishness are such as to make Jews wonder about themselves, about their friends, about the university. Against this background of doubts, questionings, and insecurity, the student interprets the friendly gesture of the registrar, the frown of the dormitory counselor. He finds himself oscillating between proof and disproof of his preconceptions. Never quite sure, he is thrust back upon his original suspicions.

Students, like their fathers and mothers, like all human beings whose freedom of mobility is limited, strive to bypass the barriers that limit their freedom. They try to overcome the stigma they think is attached to the name. By virtue of that name, they all—rich and poor, organized and unorganized —share a common awareness, frequently a self-conscious awareness of the world outside their community. The gentiles are a problem to them, or they are a problem to the gentiles. In either case, they have become a problem to themselves. And the gentiles are central to their adjustment, crucial to their peace of mind. Hence they try consciously or unconsciously to appease the gentiles and are at pains to justify their ways before them.

The means they employ to achieve security or at least diminish the threat to their own security and the devices forced upon them by what they have come to consider a hostile environment are an unflattering commentary both upon the status of the modern Jew and higher education in America.

What are these methods? What are the drives that motivate their behavior? How do they affect the work of a Hillel director whose function is to counsel and guide Jewish students? What bearing do the questions which confront him have upon the complex problem of Jewish education in America? These questions require further exploration. This much is clear, however. The problem of Jewishness as an actual or supposed stigma goes beyond the question of ignorance of Jewish tradition or threat to Jewish culture and religion. It touches upon the crucial questions of human personality and human integrity. And as such it must become the concern of all—Jews and non-Jews alike—who are interested in the morale and well-being of a significant portion of American youth on our campuses.

Unpublished manuscript, 1944.

We shall best be able to address ourselves to the question of the religion of the Jewish student if, at the outset, we define our meaning of *religion*. In using this term, I refer to the Jewish student's theological concerns; his participation in worship as a mode of communion with God; his observance of *mitzvot;* his study of Jewish religion to attain religious clarity; and generally his vision of himself and his conduct—personal and social—as related to Jewish religious teachings.

Of course, in order to be defined as religious, a Jewish student must not necessarily be involved in all or most of these aspects. But they are the criteria I have in mind when I attempt to analyze the religion of the Jewish student. My list does not include membership in Jewish organizations, contributions to Jewish causes, leadership in Jewish temples or youth groups and the like. These activities may be, but are not necessarily, indications of Jewish religious identity.

This point was again brought home to me recently by a Jewish freshman student who had been a leading member of the confirmation class of a well-known synagogue in New York, serving as editor of its Sunday school bulletin. But on entering the university, he listed his religious preference as "agnostic."

We can perhaps clarify the religious attitudes of Jewish students today if we compare them to the attitudes of our students twenty-five years ago. In those days (when I began my work as Hillel director at Cornell) the word *Jew*, whether religious or secular, had an almost ghostly quality of terror for a considerable number of Jews. They felt it was a badge of shame. It was a source of self-consciousness and excessive sensitivity.

In those days Orthodoxy was considered a vestige or a sign of immigrant background and identity. Reform [Judaism] was a status symbol, a real or imagined indication of social and economic position as institutionalized in certain fraternity memberships. Rarely would someone think of it as a response to the challenges of modernity. Jewish religion—like religion generally—was considered outmoded, especially among the Jewish intellectuals and socially conscious university avant garde.

I remember how envious I used to be of the small but committed Christian groups on campus that clustered about the YMCA and YWCA. Those were the days of social action on campus, spearheaded by the protagonists of pacifism and radical doctrine. I was impresed by the small Christian groups whose relationship to the student peace movement or to socialism seemed dictated by Christian commitment. They saw their work on the picket lines and in demonstrations as a Christian imperative. It was their way of being Christian. Their protest against the religion of their elders, unlike that of most students at the university, took the form not of passive rejection but of active rebellion against its middle class expressions. They sought Christian commitment and identity in what they came to consider the core of Christian doctrine: the social gospel.

Despite the close link between the ethical and religious elements in Jewish tradition, and despite the reform emphasis on prophetic Judaism, few if any Jewish students considered their radical views an expression of a Jewish religious conviction or commitment. Jews were among the leaders of the social action projects and radical movements on campus. But their radicalism, whatever its unconscious source, was a form of rejection of, and substitution for, Judaism.

The small groups of thoughtful Jewish students who *were* concerned with Jewish ideas and problems sought in Judaism not *religion* but substitutes for it. Those who were observant [Orthodox] tried to find reasons, other than religious, for their practices. They derived their rationale for Jewish being from Zionism, secularism, and a humanist version of Reconstructionism.

Compared to the 1930's, we today sense a marked change in the religious climate of the university. This change has its roots in the social and political history of our time. Religion has acquired a new respectability, if only for purposes of self-identification and discussion. As for Jewish religion, the sense of shame, squeamishness, and hypersensitivity of earlier generations is giving way to a rather natural, matter-of-fact acceptance of Jewish religious identity.

However, these facts, like the membership statistics of our synagogues, tell us scarcely anything about the true state of Jewish religion in the university setting. A check mark on a religious preference card is not necessarily a declaration of faith. In the social and academic setting of today, it is easy to check the box marked "Jewish" on the university's church preference card. And it is just as easy for the son—as it was for the father—to remain oblivious to the claims and obligations of the *voluntarily* claimed faith and fate.

Even for those who have some knowledge of Jewish religion, Judaism, as idea or as experience, presents no challenge. It offers them little guidance or direction. It sets no goals which have a claim upon their hearts and minds and which define the unique insights and ways of Judaism. Thousands of young Jews belong to synagogue organizations and to Hillel Foundations, but what does membership in these groups mean to them? Most of them exhaust their Jewish interest in attending meetings, running for office, rushing from one committee room to another, playing ping-pong, and eating bagels and lox. If I may digress for a moment, I should like to point out to you that bagels and lox do not represent food: they represent a concept, an American-Jewish concept, a way of Jewish living that seems to exhaust the "religious" identity of large numbers of Jews. And this applies to students as well.

Unfortunately, most Jewish students make few demands upon the intellectual and religious tradition of Judaism. Too many of them have been satisfied with little gifts and minor answers. An Israeli folk-song, a Jewish joke, Jewish delicatessen seem to be more appreciated than the insights of Judaism about the nature of God and man. The discovery of the latter would require study and critical understanding. Above all, it would require a searching restlessness of heart and mind which would drive young people to make the effort to discover in Judaism and Jewish identity a sense of role as Jews and human beings.

There are indications, however, that some students are now making the effort. I don't mean to suggest that there is a rush to study Torah. But there are students—their numbers, I dare say, are increasing—who want to find the meaning of Jewish religion beyond the clichés and superficialities of Sunday school, confirmation, and Bar Mitzvah orations. There are serious and concerned young men and women who are eager for a first-hand contact with a biblical text. Some go so far as to ask for a naked text, unadorned and unapplied homiletically. They want to discover for themselves the living faith as implied in Scripture. Most students who come to lectures, discussions, or courses in Jewish religion still confess to just an academic interest in the subject matter. But as you listen to their questions you cannot help but feel that more than academic curiosity brought them to the lecture hall. They seem to seek an answer to some deeply felt personal questions; they are probing the meaning of the perennial concerns that trouble the heart and mind of growing and thoughtful young persons.

Some of these searching and concerned students have turned to Buber, Heschel, and Hasidism. Unable to attain religious "commitment," they seek to be warmed by the fires of those who have. They are accessible to the sounds and sights of tradition. [They are] willing, more than willing, to let a text, a custom, or a ceremony speak to their hearts, even if their minds cannot give assent or can only partially assent. Occasionally, they give the impression of being quite troubled and rootless. Occasionally, one gets the feeling of *pseudo*-Hasidism. Confused as their thinking and ambivalent as their sentiments may be, I find that their genuine search for an intellectually probing, inquiring religion is suffused with authentic religious sentiment.

These developments, however, have not markedly affected the attendance of students at religious services. Institutional worship, even for those who are or want to be worshipful, is more of a problem in the university setting than it is in the community at large. This much, however, seems clear: coming to Sabbath services is no longer a sign of intellectual sloppiness or social backwardness. Among those who do come to worship regularly (and often leave immediately after the service before the Oneg Shabbat) are some of the thoughtful, intellectually concerned and popular students at the university. In any case there is this saving remnant which, in spite of obstacles (I shall refer to these later), is gradually finding its way to the synagogue and Jewish religion.

What I have said thus far about the more favorable religious climate at the university, the naturalness with which most Jewish students identify themselves as religious, and the "saving remnant" may, in some ways, prove quite deceptive. For there is much in the culture of our time, and in the culture of the university in particular, that negates the historic faith of Jewish and Christian religion and its institutional expressions today. There are considerable numbers of Jewish students whose intellectual integrity and commitment to a naturalistic view prevents their claiming the easy religious identities prevalent in our society today. For them the gulf between religion and science, so characteristic of modern culture, has not been bridged. And they are far removed from Jewish religion and are even further removed from the synagogue.

True, some do retain a relationship to the Jewish community, even a filial respect for their tradition, but in their efforts at forming a philosophy of life Judaism plays no role. Their intellectual concerns may be quite broad and deep, but Judaism as intellectual or spiritual discipline is not one of their concerns. This may be due partly to their abysmal ignorance of Jewish tradition, but it is due largely to the scientific temper of the university. Insofar as they view Judaism as a religion—and there are those who have come to believe, for reasons good and bad, that it is primarily and solely a religion—they reject Judaism as they reject *all* religion.

There is yet another group. Its members do not reject

religion; they are attracted to it. But they reject Judaism. We need to know about them and speak of them more than we do. Although they are few in number—I am inclined to think their number is likely to grow—they are significant to our understanding of the problem of Jewish religion and the synagogue in our time. Like the "neo-orthodox" and the neo-Hasidim—the followers of Heschel and Buber—they stammeringly seek to affirm a relationship to the living God. But unlike those who in spite of obstacles are finding—or are seeking to find—the focus of their religious identity in the synagogue, the students in this group have ceased looking (perhaps they never did look) to Judaism for an answer to their quest.

The obstacles loom too large. What these students know of Jewish religion is the one-dimensional, organization-minded, and earthbound Jewish religious culture of today. Contemporary Judaism, in its different versions, does not, as they see it, address itself to their ultimate concerns, their human predicament, their deepest needs. It tries too hard to be relevant. It is too much concerned with the world and the Jews, too little with the agonies of lonely, confused, and rootless persons. It is too preoccupied with the social facts and factors of contemporary society. It is too far removed, in faith and form, from what these students dimly feel religion should offer.

Perhaps if they knew more about Jewish tradition in different times and places, its historic spirit and structure, they might not be so easily alienated by contemporary distortions of a great tradition. But they know too little. Their Sunday and Hebrew school training, as they recall it, seems to have consisted largely of a series of ritual words and phrases in Hebrew or English, a few ethical maxims and slogans, the early biblical tales and the latest Israeli folk songs. There is little in these to call them back to the great tradition, little that is life-giving and redemptive in what they experience and know as Jewish religion.

When science and philosophy fail them and they turn to religion, some of them seek God not in the synagogues of their fathers, but among the Quakers, the Unitarians, and others. We shall be doing them and ourselves a grave injustice if we resort to the overworked epithet: escapists. Some are no doubt escaping from Jewish fate. May it not be possible, however, that others are escaping from the barrenness of present-day Jewish faith—its hollow rituals and grandiose clichés, that they are leaving the synagogue in search of religion, a faith that will sustain them?

The youthful criticisms and judgments by these students sound and are harsh indeed, unmellowed by experience or knowledge. But they need to be taken seriously. For the "escapists," in their different varieties, often speak for many good and thoughtful Jewish students and teachers who have not escaped. They are articulating clearly what is dimly felt and is unuttered by many Jewish students and teachers, including those who, as I said earlier, are in the synagogue or are groping towards it.

What I have tried to convey in this paper can be stated very simply. The problem of Jewish religious attitudes in the university community is not essentially a problem of conventional religious identity—whether Orthodox, Conservative, or Reform. It is largely an intellectual and spiritual problem which goes beyond denominational and institutional identities. It is not peculiar to the university, the so-called "intellectual" community. But the problems arising from the encounter of religion and modern culture, including contemporary Jewish culture, often get their sharpest definitions in the university setting. Here, in the creative centers of our society and in the sensitive and responsive hearts of thoughtful and serious young men and women, Jewish religion and the synagogue are challenged as nowhere else in the country. Neither rabbis nor laymen, off-campus or on-campus, realize the seriousness of this challenge. It deserves our utmost attention.

*Delivered at seminar on
"The Jewish College Student"
at the convention of the
Central Conference of American
Rabbis, New York City,
June 23, 1961.*

Last year, we began our Foundation program with a discussion of *God and Man at Chicago*. The subject should have been *gods and men* at Chicago, for there are many gods claiming the attention and loyalty of men.

Koheleth said, "To the making of books there is no end." One might say with equal cogency, "To the making of gods there is no end." For man is by nature a god-maker, an idol worshipper.

There is idol worship in churches and synagogues when men come to be preoccupied with the means rather than the ends of religion—with ritual and ceremony, with words, and even with music—forgetting the ends and convictions which are to guide their lives.

There is idol worship in universities when the rituals of classroom and textbook—of quiz and exam—make one forget the objects of study, the objectives of education, and the good life.

The great commandment of religion is that THOU SHALT MAKE NO GRAVEN IMAGE—THOU SHALT NOT WORSHIP IDOLS. What is an idol? It is the work of a man, the work of his hands or the imagination of his heart and mind. Ultimately, the commandment against idol worship must also be part of the commitment of a university.

From remarks delivered at the B'nai B'rith Hillel Foundation at the University of Chicago, undated.

The major religious issues of our time are common to both Jews and Christians. The difficulties in the supernatural concepts of religion are reflected in the attitudes of students on campus. While a large number seem unaffected by the new information they acquire, the general atmosphere of classroom and laboratory often stimulates critical reflection on the meaning of religion. Does modern man have need of it? What is its role in our society? If the Bible is a human document, what is its place in the religious life? What is the value of tradition? Other questions concern the role of institutions in religious life. Must one affiliate with a synagogue in order to worship God? Is it not enough "just to be a good person?" These are not the most popular subjects of discussion on campus, but a considerable number of students think and talk about them.

Courses in anthropology and psychology sharpen old questions concerning God and life and death, and they add new ones. Against the elementary Sunday school concept of religion seems to be arrayed the whole apparatus of the university —its laboratories, its libraries, its courses. No wonder that the theological foundation of many a student's faith, even if secure before his coming to the university, begins to be shaken. He fights again the old battles between the Biblical story of creation and the theory of evolution, between science and religion.

Contact with Jews who differ from him in belief and orthodoxy complicates the doubts and questions precipitated by classroom and laboratory. An Orthodox Jew is often shocked, upon meeting a Reform Jew for the first time, to discover that there are Jews who neither observe the dietary laws nor wear hats in the synagogue. The other day a student engaged me in a long discussion, outwardly "academic" but actually profoundly personal. He tried to prove that only Orthodox Jews have a right to call themselves Jews. He resented the fact that people who worshipped without hats and did not observe dietary laws were referred to as Jews.

Social pressure—the desire for the approbation of the intellectually or socially fashionable—hastens changes in behavior. Some discard, with varying degrees of reluctance, old beliefs and practices. Others continue their religious observances as concessions to family loyalty or as vague sentimental attachments. Many search for new meaning, for relevant explanations of their heritage.

They all need a sympathetic counselor, someone who can sense their confusion and their inarticulate doubts, someone who can listen to them and understand their difficulties. They need a patient teacher to help them gain knowledge and a mature understanding of themselves and their faith.

In most universities, Jewish students are unlikely to find opportunities for the study of Jewish religion. Few American universities offer courses in the history and thought of Judaism. The courses that are offered deal for the most part with the religion of the Old Testament; Judaism remains an introduction to Christianity. The whole range of medieval and modern Jewish thought is almost completely omitted. This leaves the thoughtful student wondering about Jewish history and literature of the succeeding centuries, about customs and observances associated with home and synagogue. Neither the naive Judaism of his pre-college days nor the Judaism of the university classroom is adequate to give him a sense of the relevance of his tradition, of its adequacy as a religion for Jews in our time.

The Hillel Foundation therefore seeks to supplement the academic program of the university. In public lectures and group discussion, in seminars and private conferences, it introduces Jews and Christians alike to the historic development of Jewish religion and its modern expressions. It attempts to help young Jews, perplexed as to the meaning of their faith, to see their religious problems in historic perspective and guide them through knowledge to conviction.

Excerpts from unpublished manuscript, undated, but probably written 1950.

Like all educators, Hillel directors often wonder how much of an impact they make. A Hillel director is a rather lonely person. Many people come to his office, and many activities take place in his building. Yet, I have often felt that ours is a kind of anonymous immortality. Here and there we touch a young person; occasionally we manage to say something which somebody may remember many years later. But most of the time we do not like to be anonymous. Like all human beings we need the assurance that what we do has meaning and establishes a relationship between us and others which may lead to new insights and new understandings. Therefore, the Summer Institute is for us not just an experiment in education, although it is that, too, but an opportunity to discover more fully and concretely what the values and commitments are which should be central in our lives as well as in our activities on campus. . . .

Last Saturday night, we opened the *Slichot* [1] season preceding our High Holidays. Our *Slichot* prayers contain a

1. "Penitential Prayers." Special type of prayer requesting God's mercy and forgiveness for sin, recited before Rosh Hashanah and Yom Kippur.

remarkable sentence: "Righteousness is Thine, O Lord; confusion is ours." Our confusion arises from the fact that we are human. We are baffled by the immensity of the questions about God and man and purpose which confront every human being and with which we have wrestled during this Institute. Who can ultimately answer these questions?

I do not believe we came here to discover what the Sabbath means, even though the Sabbath was our theme. I think we did not even come here to find out what Judaism means. I believe we came here to discover what our lives mean. We came to search for some understanding of man's perennial questions: Who am I? And what is my place in this mysterious and bewildering world? In reviewing the foundations of our own tradition as embodied in the Sabbath, we have tried to discover some of the answers to these questions. For ultimately we are concerned with how man—any man, Jewish man—can find sustenance, meaning, and support in our Jewish tradition for his answer to these questions.

The [Hillel] summer institute is designed to raise these deep and profound questions. And now at the end of this week's experience, you may wonder: how can we take what we found here back with us and communicate it? How can we make it meaningful? Here we studied the Sabbath; we lived and experienced it. Yet in the world outside most people do not know *Shabbat*. How can we, wherever we are going, fulfill our function to transform the world into a *Shabbat*?

Those who are in search of faith and commitment must find something which will help them sense and create *Shabbat* around themselves. They must seek knowledge and understanding. They must learn to immerse themselves in study. They need to discover a sense of relationship to those who preceded them. They must learn to extend themselves in time and must begin to sense that Abraham, Isaac, and Jacob are not just names but part of that procession of generations affirming those human ideals which speak to the needs of man and to the concerns of Jews as human beings.

I hope you will always find yourself in that procession.

Excerpts from conclud-
ing statement, National
Hillel Summer Institute,
Camp B'nai B'rith,
Starlight, Pennsylvania,
September 4, 1961.

CHANGING PATTERNS OF JEWISH LIFE
ON THE CAMPUS

A few days ago, the daily paper of one of our state universities carried an inconspicuous story reporting that a well-known midwestern university would not permit freshmen students to engage in student activities before the second quarter of their first school year. The same issue of the paper reported that the "Christ the King Foundation" of the Episcopal Church was planning to establish a college in cooperation with the University of Chicago. This college would share the facilities of the university, but its educational objectives and curriculum would be Christian in orientation.

These two news items point to significant changes in the intellectual and religious climate of our universities. Extra-curricular activities have been a major concern of students and university administrators in many schools. To a large degree, they have also affected the tone, character, and constituency of religious organizations on campus. Now however, in many schools there is a growing tendency to discourage these activities. Increased emphasis on study, research, and intellectual achievement has reduced student participation in once-popular activities and is relegating them to a position of minor importance on campus.

The Episcopal Church's decision to enlarge and intensify

its intellectual activities at the university is part of a growing concern among Christian university workers with the alienation from their religious traditions of many of the best minds in our society. They recognize that one can no longer hope to capture the interest of intelligent and thoughtful students through "activities"—the hayrides and barn dances of the YMCA and YWCA, the picnics of the early Hillel Foundations, the whole gamut of activities which attracted hundreds of students to the different religious foundations at the university. In their stead, on many campuses a more serious and consistent effort is now being made to engage the mind and imagination of the thoughtful student and to confront him with the reality of religion and its relevance for his life.

The situation was quite different thirty or forty years ago when the Hillel Foundation initiated its work at American universities. The campus was dominantly activity-centered. The means of education which were used during the early years of Hillel's existence grew out of the setting and climate of the university. With a sure grasp of the spirit and structure of the campus, Hillel too used the activity-centered method to involve students in the Hillel program and to give them a sense of at-homeness in the Foundation. Hillel's open forums and courses of study, choral and dance groups and religious celebrations, the Hillel theater and debating teams at Illinois, Michigan, Ohio State, and other schools, gave Hillel's name campus-wide prestige and made the collective name *Jew* a source of pride and stimulus to Jewish identity for many half-frightened and some self-hating Jews. Many who had previously denied their identity came out of their hiding places in the gilded ghettos of the fraternities or the activity-centered "Y" 's. Gradually, they began to rediscover their own name and learned to pronounce it.

The Frankels and the Sachars who pioneered the Hillel idea and method in our universities and gave it shape and substance, saw in Hillel a movement designed to return generations of college men and women to the Jewish fold. They knew they were engaged in a mission of rescue, both human and Jewish. They knew they were helping the sons and daughters of ghetto dwellers or their children to rediscover their human worth and American dignity in the inner security that can spring from a meaningful and satisfactory experience of Jewishness.

Hundreds of Jewish students were involved in the Foundation's activities every week, and Hillel became known as "a home away from home" for Jewish students. What by now has turned into a cliché was a correct and comprehensive description of Hillel's work and spirit at that time. Hillel Foundations were indeed homes away from home on many campuses. They helped Jewish students find warmth, fellowship, and a sense of at-homeness in a setting in which the social and psychological effects of their underprivileged position were quite real and often painful. The campus population in those days was predominantly non-Jewish. The Jewish student body was small, largely made up of sons of immigrants or of immigrants themselves. The lines of demarcation between Christian and Jewish fraternities were sharply defined; the YMCA was the dominant campus religious institution and sponsored the freshman orientation week and similar activities. In this setting, being Jewish meant being strange; it meant not being wholly at home in the world or in the campus community. The frightened, half-frightened, or insecure Jew seeking to gain an American nativity or identity discovered a sense of at-homeness in the Hillel Foundation.

We must also remember that East European Jews and German Jews in the American Jewish community were still sharply divided in those days. The campus fraternities reflected this division and often added refinements to it. The Hillel Foundation served as a home and refuge for many students who would not or could not join fraternities. Within the Hillel Foundation, fraternity men and independents who joined in common interest and activities were molded into a united Jewish student community.

Today, the campus situation has changed considerably. Hundreds of thousands of Jewish students are at our universities. They are third-generation Americans and are at home in America. There is no sense of underprivileged position. There is no quota system. Fraternities, the former strongholds of prejudice, are becoming nonsectarian. True, there are still "Jewish" and "gentile" fraternities, but the sharp lines of demarcation are gradually disappearing. Jews can be found in proportionately large numbers both in all areas of student life and on the faculty. Being Jewish has generally become an acceptable and respectable identity on campus. It certainly has lost the stigma attached to it in former days by Jew-haters or Jewish self-haters. Moreover, religion also has acquired a new respectability, as a form of identity for the many and as a subject for serious intellectual and personal inquiry for the few. This applies to Jews as well as non-Jews. At any rate, the Jewish student's hypersensitivity and his reluctance to affirm his identity openly are fast disappearing.

These changes have considerable bearing on the future role and function of the Hillel Foundations. Let me list some of their implications for our work.

(1) In a free and democratic university setting in which Jews constitute a sizable segment of the student population, the need for kinship and Jewish fellowship will increasingly lose its importance as a major stimulus to Jewish community life on campus. The new trends in university housing emphasize the social function of the dormitories: every dormitory has its own lounge where students can get together. In the words of one student, every dormitory now has a little Hillel social center within it. Hillel's function as a socializing agent for Jewish students will diminish steadily.

(2) Today's students are no longer reluctant to affirm their Jewishness. But in most instances they are ignorant of what they affirm. Moreover, the little they know of Judaism is not always sufficiently attractive to make their affirmation whole-hearted. Our central problem today is no longer that Jewish students try to escape from Judaism. The problem is that Judaism is escaping them. Some of our most sensitive and thoughtful students feel that Judaism does not address itself to their concerns and predicaments as human beings, as human-beings-born-Jews, in our time. It does not engage their minds even while it superficially engages their hearts.

(3) Untroubled by majority-group social pressures and the threat of anti-Semitism and their attendant self-consciousness, Jewish students will turn to the Hillel Foundation in a significant way only if it can make Jewish knowledge and Jewish religion relevant to their concerns as troubled human beings in today's world.

(4) The Hillel Foundation will have to decide just whom it is addressing. We must establish priorities. We cannot serve everybody. We may as well face this fact. But if we cannot serve everybody, to whom will one director on a campus with thousands of Jewish students be able to address himself? To whom should he address himself—to the thoughtful ones? to the future artists, the future writers, philosophers, professors —to whom?

There are still other questions which require clarification. If we are going to engage students in an intellectual dialogue within the universe of knowledge which is a university, who is best qualified for this task and how can this task be accomplished? Is a Hillel director always the best-equipped or most appropriate person for this job? Or would a Chair of Jewish Studies be a more appropriate way?

Or think of our Hillel houses which often represent investments of substantial amounts. It is possible that they may not be attended in the future to the same degree they have been in the past. Instead of investing substantial funds in the establishment and maintenance of buildings, might it not be wiser to invite an outstanding scholar to, say, the University of Chicago for six weeks under the auspices of Hillel and in partnership with the university, to lecture and teach at the university and at the Hillel Foundation? Paul Tillich has been brought to the University of Chicago by Christian groups for six weeks every year, and in these six weeks Jewish students are more profoundly affected by Paul Tillich than they may be affected by the Hillel program in four years. In planning for the future, the Hillel Foundations must begin to think seriously in terms of visiting professorships, lectureships, and chairs of Jewish studies, in order to supplement, and in some instances substitute for, existing Hillel Foundations. I do not think that necessary changes should be avoided because of our investments in buildings. In order to fulfill our tasks adequately, we may have to develop other instruments of communication.

We must face this grim reality if we are engaged in the search for a new educational vision for Jewish students. And we must be concerned not only with students. Young faculty people are also waiting. Many of them are eager to learn. They no longer manifest the same antagonism to Jewishness which we found at Cornell or Michigan or Illinois thirty or forty years ago. But here, too, the question is: What will engage and involve them? And what kind of an encounter can we present to them?

There is another problem. Many universities are now introducing courses in the history and literature of religion. The Lilly Foundation recently made a grant to the University of Chicago for a study of the place of religion in the curriculum, and several distinguished committees have worked on this project. I had a chance to appear before one of the committees, and I think its members believe Judaism should not be taught merely as a preparation for Christianity but should be treated objectively, as a major religious tradition in the Western world. Yet the problem of communication is still unresolved. How do we communicate this immense tradition —three thousand years of Jewish history—in a curriculum designed for two college quarters? How do we distinguish what is more important from what may be less important in order to condense this complex matter sufficiently into the the few hours available for its study?

I think the Hillel Foundation is the logical institution to help universities develop programs of this kind or to serve them in an advisory capacity. More and more universities will be including· religion in their curriculum in the near future. We should have commissions to study the problem of curricula and methods of communication. We should explore and determine what kind of textbooks, syllabi, and reading resources we should have or should produce in order to communicate Judaism adequately at the university level.

We also should have a commission on the arts. We celebrate the Jewish holidays in our Foundations. Our holiday observances are one way in which we engage students not only in the religious but also the aesthetic dimensions of Jewish life. But we can conceivably do much more. Young people on our campuses contribute their writings to all kinds of magazines, yet rarely to a Hillel publication. They write books and plays, but we are not the text, the subject matter they think or write about. Perhaps we can stimulate a budding composer, artist, or poet to respond creatively to the experience of his Jewishness and to transform his Jewish commitment into a significant contribution to Jewish thought and life. The Hillel Foundation can conceivably become one of the great instruments for creative expression of Jewish life.

Finally, I think we must utilize the summer more than we have done in the past. Jewish education in the United States has come to recognize the importance of the summer for educational purposes. Throughout the year, time and space are determined by the dominant culture, even in the best Hillel Foundations. The time and the space of the students, the symbols of the world they live in, are part of the dominant civilization. Jewishness, so to speak, is squeezed in—and squeezed out—as students rush from one activity and classroom to another. The summer gives us a unique opportunity to control the time and space of students for educational purposes. Our experience in our annual summer institutes tells us something about the possibilities of a summer program. Right now our summer institute lasts only eight days. Suppose we had an institute not of eight days but eight weeks! Suppose we invited some of the young poets, the young dramatic talent, the young painters, writers, and musicians we have on campus, and brought them together with outstanding artists and writers who have Jewish interests and commitments and with professors of theology and philosophy who have shown an interest and competence in Jewish thought and life? In this kind of setting we could do something for these young people which could not be matched or duplicated anywhere else. A more extensive and imaginative utilization of the summer is one of the great tasks we shall have to undertake in the near future.

I know these projects and plans will require substantial funds. Christ the King Foundation, when it thinks of its program, is thinking in terms of twenty million dollars and even larger amounts. I do not know whether we shall ever be able to think in such terms. However, I know the members of the National Hillel Commission are just as concerned with these problems as are the members of Hillel's professional staff. I realize that a sense of concern alone will not raise funds, but it seems to me that with concern we can move in the proper direction. And I believe our problem is not merely the problem of any one "commission" or single organization; what is at stake is the American Jewish community. Indeed, what is at stake is not only the American

Jewish community but also Judaism in our time. Can it engage in this intellectual dialogue with the world? Does it have to say something to the world? Does it have something to say to Jews—not something parochial or therapeutic to relieve them of a feeling of inferiority or insecurity but something to give them a sense of purpose and role as both Jews and human beings?

The Hillel Foundations stand at the center of the stage on which the drama of the Jewish encounter with the Christian world and intellectual trends of our time is taking place. Our future depends on our ability and that of B'nai B'rith to measure up to the opportunities and responsibilities inherent in our position. We hope we shall succeed with your help and the cooperation of the American Jewish community.

Presented as part of a symposium on "Changing Patterns of Jewish Life on the Campus" at the annual meeting of the B'nai B'rith Hillel Commission, Washington, D.C., November 13, 1960.

PERSONAL CONVICTION AND
INSTITUTIONAL OBJECTIVES

At a conference of Hillel directors several years ago, some colleagues raised a question which I consider crucial to our work as rabbis and Hillel directors. They asked for an examination of the conflicts which may arise between a man's personal convictions and his institutional responsibilities.

Their concern was triggered by the rules which the administrators of our Hillel Summer Institute for Student Leaders had introduced to govern the observance of the Sabbath at the institute. Some men—among them not only Reform Jews —maintained that a policy which prevented a man from observing the Sabbath in the light of his personal convictions should not be promulgated by institutional decision. Others argued that the nature of a Hillel Foundation required an administrative decision which would guide Sabbath observance and similar practices everywhere in Hillel.

In the course of these discussions, I formulated the premise that whenever there is conflict between preference and conviction, conviction is to take precedence. I based this formulation on the following considerations:

(1) The Hillel Foundation aims to be the all-inclusive Jewish community on the campus.

(2) That it may be inclusive, it must provide a sense of

at-homeness to Jewish students of different backgrounds and beliefs.

(3) Since the breaking of the Sabbath does violence to the conviction of those who observe it, it limits their sense of at-homeness in the Hillel Foundation. By limiting this sense of at-homeness, it negates the aim of inclusiveness. Therefore, we insist that in the larger interests of inclusiveness, conviction takes precedence whenever there is a conflict between conviction and preference.

Even though I know that this approach raises as many questions as it may answer, I believe it enables us to formulate a clear position on the question of observance in the Hillel Foundation. The decisions of the Hillel director with reference to Sabbath observance, *kashrut*, and similar *mitzvot*— although based on *halakhah* or in harmony with it—cannot necessarily be viewed as halakhic decisions, nor can either students or others be asked to comply with them in the name of *halakhah*. As the union of the diverse, the Hillel Foundation cannot represent one point of view with reference to *halakhah*. Given the diversity of belief within it and within the Jewish community, the Hillel Foundation is neither authorized nor capable of legislating for all—in their diversities—in the name of any one concept of Jewish religion in our time, be it Orthodox, Conservative, or Reform. For it cannot represent any one religious position to the exclusion or detriment of the others.

Consequently, the Hillel director as rabbi, as *dayan*,[1] cannot serve as the rabbi of all the members or religious groups within the Hillel Foundation except by the consent of the governed. Since the consent of the different religious groups is, by definition, impossible, we must assume that the rabbinic functions and powers of the Hillel director are, generally speaking, limited to those whose religious beliefs or denomination are like his. He may well be respected by all; he may

1. "Judge." Member of a rabbinical court.

be the teacher of all. But he cannot be the rabbi and *dayan* for all—Orthodox, Conservative, Reform, Reconstructionist —alike. Only as the director of the Foundation, as the community manager, does his jurisdiction extend over all groups within the Foundation. As such he is concerned with the unity and inclusiveness of the community, and he tries to arrive at a decision which would prove reasonable to all who are *equally* concerned with the unity of the community and the at-homeness of its diverse groups.

The function of the director becomes at the same time his somber, almost permanent predicament, namely, to make possible the community of the different in a setting and in a spirit conducive to the maintenance and development of both *community* and *difference*. How to orchestrate the different with no or little violence to the component units making up the inclusive community constitutes the essential problem of the Hillel director. What are the principles by which he can be guided in this orchestration?

It is at this point that we come face to face with the director's personal convictions. For even though his dominant function as Hillel director is that of educator and community director, as rabbi, by his training and commitment as rabbi, he represents certain convictions on the fundamental questions of Jews and Judaism. He may rightly feel that his rabbinic mission (if we may use this term) cannot be just to orchestrate differences, but to articulate the difference he represents, his convictions, his beliefs. He will of course be aware of his responsibility to those who are different from him; he will be conscious of their needs and interests, but can he with integrity slur over his commitments as Conservative, Orthodox, Reform, or Reconstructionist, his Zionist or non-Zionist orientation?

How then can or will he serve all those who differ from him, as he must as director of the Hillel community? More important, can he serve them all equally? Consider, for instance, the problem of religious services. If he directs a Foundation whose students have not articulated their religious preferences, what kind of religious service will he offer? Is not the fact that he is an Orthodox, Conservative, or Reform rabbi likely to affect his Foundation's mode of worship or choice of prayerbook? If he decides to have different kinds of services for the different denominations in his Foundation, is it not likely (if not inevitable) that the main service will be that conducted by the director while the others will be additional services conducted by a student or faculty member? Are we not called upon to ask ourselves the question—indeed to examine our conscience—whether we have not often allowed our own convictions to become institutional preferences?

Or consider Hillel's cultural program. Students of course share in its making, but the director's influence is decisive in most instances. How much room will there be in the program for, let me say, the discussion of Israel? Will not a director's convictions and preferences, his being a Zionist or non-Zionist, affect the answer considerably? I am not suggesting that it can be otherwise. I am merely trying to indicate how complex the theory and practice of community inclusiveness are and how difficult it is to maintain and develop the religious difference a student brings with him to the university.

We must further assume that the director of the Hillel Foundation not only provides religious or cultural services but is himself a "service" as the leader who embodies certain qualities, certain influences, certain values. His religious integrity as Orthodox, Conservative, or Reform rabbi, his commitment to social issues, his views on Israel, are inseparable from the "bias" which he as a person embodies. This "bias"—mostly subconscious yet conscious at times—quite frequently may become the bias of the Foundation.

Students have written to our national administration protesting that their Foundation was dominantly Orthodox,

Reform, or Zionist. It should be pointed out parenthetically that it is not necessarily the conviction or preference of the director that shapes the character of a Foundation. Quite often the students he works with—the nucleus he has managed to attract—will give a specific definition to his Foundation. Inevitably those in opposing camps will feel, rightly or wrongly, that the Foundation is "run" by the Orthodox, the Zionist, or the Reform students. Regardless of the truth of such feelings, what about those who are not Zionist or Orthodox or Conservative or Reform? Are we serving them dominantly or, if I may say so, recessively? Don't they, by the inclusive Hillel definition, have the right to equal considerations, understanding, and affection?

Closely related to this question of inclusiveness is another even more fundamental question. What is the inclusiveness to which we refer when we speak of our concern with *k'lal Yisrael*—the totality of Judaism? Whom and what does it exclude? Inasmuch as we, in the Hillel Foundation, must inevitably be selective in the transmission of the heritage of the past, what are the principles of selection? Whom and what do we include or exclude, and on what basis? These questions are, of course, not peculiar to us as Hillel directors. They are of crucial concern to all who profess to teach Judaism. I mention them here only to emphasize again how careful we must be in our use of such words as inclusiveness or totality.

This, then, is the predicament of the Hillel director as a rabbi and as a person. He has been assigned an almost impossible task: to build the *community* of the *different*. Can he serve all and serve them equally? How can he do it?

The arrangements governing inter-religious activities at Cornell University may provide a possible answer. The Cornell United Religious Work is an institution which seeks to serve all Christians at Cornell University. Similar institutions exist on other campuses. The director of CURW is the administrative head of an interfaith organization in which each minister serves the students of his denomination—a Methodist minister serves the Methodist student center, the Catholic is in charge of the Catholic student program, the Congregationalist works with the students of his denomination, and the rabbi directs the Hillel program. The activities common to all groups are planned and done jointly; those not in common are done separately. There is greater emphasis on the separate activities of each group than on common activities. In addition, provision is made for a nondenominational or interdenominational Society of Christian Students.

I am not trying to indicate that the Christian situation is parallel to ours. Some may feel that the approach represented by the Cornell United Religious Work has little to suggest to us. Others may insist that the Hillel Foundation's function is not, or should not be, the perpetuation of religious divisions —Orthodox, Conservative, Reform—that exist in the community, but should be the training of students towards a new religious synthesis. This may be a desirable goal. Many of us feel our present religious divisions do not contribute much to religious clarity or expression. But if this be our goal and task, new questions arise. Would it not be our moral obligation to tell our students, their parents, and, indeed, the entire Jewish community what our intentions are? Would it not be our obligation to state publicly that the Hillel rabbi, regardless of his background, represents a new type, a new synthesis, that he is not the orchestrator of differences within the Foundation but the protagonist of a new concept of Judaism which the Hillel program is designed to express and further?

The questions I have raised are not an academic exercise. They are eminently practical. They touch upon our relations both with persons who come under our influence and with those we wish to attract. They relate to our essential function as teachers and community servants, as rabbis and spokesmen of the institution we serve. How can we best serve our students? How can we serve them equally—given our human frailty, our personal bias, our personal convictions? How can we speak our minds with integrity on religion, social problems, or even political issues, yet not allow our voice to be heard as "the voice of the Hillel Foundation"?

These are not easy questions, nor are they peculiar to us. But it is our responsibility to ask them again and again, and by asking to be led to that self-examination that will make us more deeply aware of our goals and give us the humility we must have in the difficult tasks that are ours.

Delivered at the annual
conference of Hillel
Directors, Camp B'nai B'rith,
Starlight, Pennsylvania,
August 23, 1954.

Notes

Part 4

and Reflections

It is extremely difficult for me to represent my class at this time. Only an hour or two ago, I might have represented it in the capacity of student; now it is my privilege to speak for it as a rabbi during the first moments of his rabbinic ministry. These first moments, despite their tremendous significance as dramatizations of the end of a period in our lives, are not, alas, sufficiently miraculous to transform us immediately into what we are to become only after many years of experience, further study, and contemplation. For I view the ministry not as a state of being, but rather as a process of becoming, ever working and striving to attain the full meaning of a teacher and leader in Israel that makes us dare assume—in spite of our failings and shortcomings—the title of rabbi, and with it the challenge so eloquently and inspiringly presented by Dr. Wise this morning.

Every generation likes to think of itself as facing the most critical moment in history and as being called upon to solve the most difficult problems of the age. Yet it seems to me we are not entirely incorrect in assuming the critical character of our time for Israel and the world. Amidst the economic and social disintegration, the political confusion and spiritual homelessness of our age, the rabbi must discover a way to lead his people to meaningful Jewish and human living. At a time when Jewish life, insofar as it exists at all in any given community, is limited to the four walls of the synagogue, it is the task of the rabbi to widen the domain of Jewishness, to extend its influence over the whole of life. In an age when church and synagogue, despite their protestations of social justice, are predominantly on the side of those who *have* rather than on the side of those who *have not*, the rabbi, if he is to be true to his mission, must strive to help bring the realities of existence in harmony with the spirit of Jewish tradition. These are indeed difficult tasks. If our ministry is to have any effectiveness or meaning for ourselves and our communities, we shall have to face them honestly, face them, however, not as subjects for sermons, but as challenges to action.

Life today, with its woes and sorrows, its misery and starvation, requires action. The world has had too much of words, especially of pious, religious words. . . . It gasps and bleeds in a sea of words. Some day it may indeed be drowned —the danger of another deluge is not yet over in spite of the promise of God to Noah, and ministers of religion will have contributed not a little to the catastrophe, should it come.

The dominant role played by words in the synagogue of today can be traced partly to the verbalization of Judaism by the Reform movement. Reform Judaism, in its attempt to bring Jewish tradition in harmony with reason, robbed Judaism of some of its most vital institutions, customs, and ceremonies, and substituted for them verbalizations and formulae such as monotheism, the mission of Israel, and social justice. Syllogisms and logical formulae are verbal, but much of Jewishness and religion is psychological rather than logical—

complex patterns of rites, customs, and habits which have become deeply imbedded in the soul of our people and form part of the dynamics of Jewish life.

If Judaism is to regain its varied richness of content we shall have to reinstate action and feeling in Jewish life and, in terms of these two elements, reintroduce a new discipline of customs, habits and ceremonies in our individual and collective life. The task is enormously difficult. We lack the necessary milieu, the folk-life out of which the re-creation and redynamization of some of our traditional folkways can spring. But this old-new discipline is a basic need, and we must work towards it.

In this reinterpretation and redynamization of Jewish folkways we may look to Palestine for inspiration and guidance. Its Oneg Shabbat and its Purim festival, its songs and dances can serve as stimuli and guides in our creative attempts. And Zionism can, if acted upon, help us to work out a more adequate concept of Jewish life in America—only, however, if we remove from it the beggar's badge of shame we have placed upon it, and allow its spirit to master our hearts and minds. Then will we substitute for speeches and sermons on the glory of *Haluzim* a program of adult Jewish education; then will Hebrew become an integral part of our educational system; then will Hebrew literature assume a greater role in our lecture programs and forums. Palestine and Zionism will have rooted themselves in the American Jewish community.

If we do this, we shall be ready for the conquest of the Jewish community and the consolidation of world Jewry. Jewish unity, so much discussed and so urgently needed, seems to be the flowering of Jewish sorrow and misery. It is negative. Jewish unity will become creative only when the negative forces which bring it about are supplanted by the desire not only to defend and protect suffering Jews, but to enrich and ennoble Judaism everywhere, including our own land.

Address delivered at graduation from Jewish Institute of Religion, New York City, June 4, 1933.

REMARKS ON ROSH HASHANAH EVE

W̶e have gathered to celebrate the beginning of another year. Millions of Jews all over the world will welcome it with prayer and song tonight. Yet as you walked towards this synagogue, you could not have noticed any change in the world about you. The setting sun colored the horizon today as it did yesterday and the day before. The stars in the sky evinced no change of mood, and the darkness that is enveloping the earth is no different from that which preceded it or will follow it. Nature does not recognize the new years and new year celebrations of man. Time flows on eternally. It knows no limitations, no boundaries, no measurements, no gradations. The earth today revolves around its axis and around the sun in the self-same manner that it did thousands of years ago, when Moses stood at Sinai, when Isaiah preached his immortal prophecies, when Socrates strolled along the streets of Athens.

Time knows no limitation. But man, limited and finite, divides it and designates each particle of time by a special name—a minute, an hour, a month, a year. For him each one of the earth's revolutions around the sun is different from the preceding one, each cycle of three hundred and sixty-five days presents a sum different from that of the past or the future. He measures time in terms of events, in terms of experience. And each day or month or year assumes significance through the experience associated with it. Sorrow and joy, love and hate, hope and futility, aspiration and disappointment, birth and death—these are the elements out of which man's days are compounded. And each of them glorifies and sanctifies certain days—some we remember as days of joy, others as days of sadness.

As it is with individuals, so it is with peoples. They too, in the course of their history, come to associate certain events with certain days and to identify some of their experiences and the ideals growing out of them with particular dates in the year. We call these days which symbolize the experiences of a people holidays or holy days. A holiday is the dramatized expression of a people's experience, of its relationship to man, to nature, and to God. As the experiences of people vary, so do the symbolic expressions of those experiences. And it is the difference in the character of those expressions which give us a clue to the nature of those peoples—their ideals, their ideas, their points of view. All peoples celebrate the new year. The changes in the seasons evoke certain sentiments and moods in all peoples. But how differently they express these moods and sentiments. Think of the manner in which Christians celebrate the new year and compare that to the spirit permeating Jewish homes and synagogues all over the world tonight. Think of the seriousness and earnestness which characterize our celebration of Rosh Hashanah, of the humble penitence and the devout prayerfulness which usher in this holy day.

The rabbis tell us that Rosh Hashanah marks the creation of the first man upon the earth. "It was on Rosh Hashanah, in the first hour of that day, that the thought came to God to create Adam, the first human being." Jewish tradition neither associates the Jewish new year with the birth of a particular person—the father of our people—nor does it commemorate

the greatness of Jewish heroes. It signifies the birth of man—
man in the first days of creation, a nameless, nationless creature—Adam. Out of dust did God create him, out of the dust
of all the earth. This is the rabbinic concept of man's origin.
Not from the dust of Jerusalem, the holy city, nor from the
earth of Palestine, the cradle of Israel, nor from the shores
of the Rhine was man created. But from every corner of the
earth, east and west, north and south, dust was gathered to
create man. And the rabbis explain this act of God as an
indication of the equality of men wherever they may be,
whatever the country of their birth. No nation can claim
superiority over another nation because of man's origin there.
No nation may boast of greater glory because Adam the
father of mankind belonged to its nationality. . . . "And in the
image of God created He man," the biblical narrative tells
us. Equal in origin and equal before God. The divine glory
of God shines upon all human beings alike. They all face
the same creator. They all are created in His image.

This is the Jewish concept of man's origin as associated
with Rosh Hashanah. It is a concept which the world has
not yet accepted. More than ever, the superiority of one
people over another, of one type of humanity over another
is emphasized. The dust of one country is proclaimed superior
to the dust of another country. Some peoples are still rele-
gated to serfdom and slavery while others are given the right
to trample upon all that is dear to them. Man's basic equality
is denied by new theorists and new dictators.

Yet Rosh Hashanah, which we usher in tonight, is the
festival of the equality of man. Tonight Jews will again
emphasize this rejected concept of humanity, and we join
with them prayerfully and hopefully. We know the world
is against us and the ideals which we represent. Hitlerist
Germany, Fascist Italy, and their cohorts in the United
States and elsewhere cannot accept this principle. But we
shall emphasize it again and again, committed to the mean-

ing of this day which is a challenge to the oppressors and enslavers of humanity. May this Rosh Hashanah give us the strength and courage to uphold, through the example of our own lives, Israel's ideal of a humanity equal before God and man.

Delivered at the B'nai B'rith Hillel Foundation, Cornell University, September 9, 1934.

It is said in the Bible that God created man in his own image. Voltaire once cynically remarked that God created man in his own image and man returned the compliment. Voltaire was right. Man creates gods in his own image. His concepts of gods reflect his highest aspirations, and his picture of heaven is a would-be picture of earth. Man invests the universe with those ideals which his experience tells him are the highest.

In this sense we could say that the Bible is a reflection of Jewish ideals and aspirations. It is neither only an account of the history of the Jews during certain periods, nor is it merely the story of their relationship to their neighbors and to themselves. Above all, it is a record of their growing spiritual knowledge and a chronicle of their ascent on the ladder to heaven.

Thus conceived, the Bible is both history and utopia—a record of Israel's past and a projection of its concept of the future. As we read about its judges and its kings; its conflicts and its wars; its laws and religious ideas as prophetic utterances concerning man, nature, and God; we encounter the highest expressions of Jewish genius envisioning a more perfect world. The prophetic utterances, the anger of the prophets and their exultation, tell us not only about the wickedness and sin of Israel. They tell us even more about Israel's concept of the world that is yet to be. They give us a picture of the world as the prophets envision it—a vision of the relationship among peoples and between man and God which has become mankind's enduring hope.

From unpublished notes, undated.

At all times there have been people who wanted to know the source of life, the beginnings of things. The stories we find in Genesis embody some of the ways in which our ancestors sought to explain the mystery. These stories reflect man's profound need to have some understanding of the world around him, some sense of the meaningfulness of things, some kinship with the forces of the world. And if at times he could find no kinship with the wild beasts and volcanic eruptions in the world of nature which surrounded him, he transcended them by establishing a sense of kinship with the God who was master of them all. He linked himself with the master of all life—God Himself. Boldly and heroically, the human imagination of early Israel attached man—this weak and frail and groping being—to the Creator and to Creation. "In the beginning God created the heavens and the earth. . . . And God said, 'let us make man in our image, in our likeness, and let him have dominion over the fish of the sea, and over the fowl of the air, and over the cattle, and over all the earth.' So God created man in His own Image; in the image of God created He him." [1]

From unpublished notes, undated.

1. Genesis 1:27.

In the dream of Jacob and the ladder we find the symbol of man's propensity to project ladders (concepts) to link himself with that which is abiding in the changing universe. For man is frail, and he searches for the security which comes from that which is strong and mighty. He is a creature of time, but he seeks identity with the timeless to explain his life and give it meaning. That is what all religion represents— a ladder towards meaning, a groping for some clue to the puzzling succession of events, of life and death, of war and peace, of despair and helplessness, of unrequited love, of disillusionment and defeat. Religion has a vision of design, a pattern of thought to explain the apparently unpatterned sequence of experiences. To use terms more popular on campus, religion is the propensity of the human species to search for a rationale or ideology which will give direction and design to its life.

For man is inexorably a creature in search of meaning. Once he has satisfied his animal needs he must have a sense of worth, continuity, and purpose. "Heaven" or "God" are names man has traditionally given to the source of worth and the ultimate meaning of life.

Men have used different ladders for reaching heaven. This

difference accounts for the variety of religious worship and practice. And some have used the ladder not so much to reach heaven—to catch a glimpse of design—as to escape from earth. It is the peculiar genius of Jewish religion that it has linked heaven and earth—its ladder, like Jacob's ladder, is set upon the earth, upon the realities of human experience, but its top reaches heaven. For the Jew, heaven does not serve as an escape but as the purpose and the program for life on earth.

From unpublished notes, undated.

One of my friends was wondering the other day whether the decision to devote this year's *kallah* [1] to Hasidism [2] was due to the recent commemorations of the bicentennial year of the death of the Baal Shem. There is some truth in that, but it is only part of the story.

Two hundred years after the Baal Shem's death we too find ourselves in the midst of a religious crisis. We are searching and groping for a new understanding, for a revitalized understanding of the sources of Jewish being. The Jewish person, insofar as he is at all concerned with the problems of Jewish religion and wants to go beyond the usual clichés of Jewish identity and Jewish consciousness, is trying to discover in Hasidism a mode of Jewish religious communion and community which he does not find in the conventional denominational expressions of Jewish religion in our time.

Beyond the verbose and verbal interpretations of Judaism and the institutional formulations of contemporary Jewish

1. General "assembly" for study purposes. The name given in Babylonia to study institutes held during the Hebrew months Elul and Adar, when students from all parts of the country assembled for intensive study at the academies of Sura and Pumbedita.

2. A religious and social movement in Judaism, founded by Israel Baal Shem Tov (1699-1761) in Volhynia and Podolia.

religion, thoughtful and sensitive men and women seek to discover not easy commitments but the profoundly shattering and healing experience of closeness to God. This is the reason why the Hasidic emphasis on the experience of God rather than a disquisition about him has appealed to many who are not capable of revolting against contemporary Judaism— because they have too little to revolt against—but who are capable of yearning and groping, of intimations of God rather than of commitment to Him.

*From introductory comments
to a program on Hasidism
sponsored by the Chicago
Board of Rabbis during its
annual Kallah, Chicago, May, 1961.*

CONCEPTUAL GUIDELINES FOR
AN UNDERSTANDING OF JEWISH HISTORY
IN THE MODERN PERIOD

1. Severance in time—the great dispersion. The great disruption in Jewish history occurred not in 70 C.E. but in 1789.

2. Historically the destruction of the Temple did not affect the Jewish self-image, the character of the historic self-definition of the Jew; it affected the space within which the definition was to work out its destiny. The destruction was part of God's plan. Shocking though it may have been as experience, it was not sudden, nor was it out of harmony with the fundamental Jewish version of the world and of Israel's role in it. It had been foretold by the prophets; it represented the punishment that was bound to come upon those who had strayed from the path of God. It was the punishment for a "chosen people" that was stubborn and unrepentant and unwilling to accept the responsibility of chosenness: living in harmony with God's will.

3. The destruction of the Temple and the exile did not affect the essential nature and character of the image the Jews had of themselves as God's people; indeed, it proved the truth of the historical image as articulated by Moses and the prophets. God is master of the universe and master of history. He chose the Jews: "And ye shall be unto Me a kingdom of priests and a holy nation." *Am* and *kadosh*

belong together. For the Jew, fullness of life requires the fullness of expression of both "holy" and "people."

4. Thus the destruction of the Temple and the exile meant
neither their renunciation of their right to the land nor a
weakening of their sense of possession even though they did
not dwell in the land. It meant severance-in-space from the
land, with attachment in time to the land in its holiness, to
the God who had given both Torah and land and had chosen
Israel as the recipient of both.

5. Their relatedness to the land was nourished by the faith
that the land would be theirs again in due time. The very
concept of exile ultimately implies return: Return to God is
prerequisite to return to the land. Exile meant remembrance
of sin and punishment, of ancient glories and of the promise
of redemption that was to come. "Because of our sins were
we exiled from our land." Exile meant a reminder of Israel's
special position among the nations as an *am kadosh* which,
when it is unfaithful to its role, must live in exile and suffer
until it beomes worthy of redemption.

6. The Hellenistic diaspora: its relationship to the classic
Jewish image as we find it in the Bible.

7. The "great dispersion" of 1789 with the breakdown of
ghetto walls and the entry of the Jews into the European
world meant the beginning of *dispersion without exile*. Modernity undermined the divine sanctions of Jewish life and
thus dissolved the historic image Jews had of themselves. The
concept of exile began to lose its meaning. Jewish history
began to be interpreted in secular categories (cf. concepts
of "exile" in Reform Judaism and Zionism as well as the
approaches of Reconstructionism and Conservative Judaism).

8. As a result, we experience the severance of the two elements of the historic self-image of *am kadosh*: "Holy" and
"people" are dissociated and redefined. "Holy" is redefined
in order to reconcile the affirmations of Jewish tradition with
the philosophical and scientific concepts and theories of mo-

dernity; "people" is transformed into an empty symbol or discarded altogether in the struggle for equality. In either case, the part is substituted for the whole.

9. Dispersion without "exile" means severance in time, discontinuity. Exile in its historic Jewish context refers to relatedness to point of origin historically and in the present. It is linked to divine cause and judgment. After the French Revolution, dispersion assumes a chance character. It is an accident occurring to those who chance to come along. It is determined by social, economic and political conditions. It is the result of historic circumstances rather than of divine plan. It is not a purposeful act; it is—modernity.

10. Classic Judaism and the sense of exile and redemption that is basic to it, function in a space-time continuum. All modern philosophies of Jewish life ultimately seek to reestablish this continuum.

Unpublished outline, June, 1962.

In the dirty, dingy ghettos, our fathers who suffered persecution and discrimination more than we do, were perfectly at home in the world. They felt secure; they were never ashamed, or evasive, or self-conscious. To be different from their neighbors, that was their pride. To be like their neighbors meant to live in homes not their own. What is to us the yoke of custom and ceremony was to them a source of security and pride. And they looked down upon their neighbors whose strength and power they conceded, but whose superiority—never. For they believed in a God who had caused them to be exiled for their sins and who, in due time, would redeem them, a God who governed the world and who had chosen Israel among the nations. And in their faith they found security, and through it willingly accepted gentile hatred and scorn.

Such was their faith, and from faith comes security, comes a feeling of at-homeness in the world. Landless they were, but not homeless; and freemen, psychologically, even though slaves. Yehuda Halevi, the great Zionist poet of medieval times, could honestly speak in the name of most Jews when he wrote: "A slave is one who is a slave of man; a free man is he who is a slave of God."

From unpublished notes, undated.

Zionists have frequently spoken of the *homelessness* of the Jewish people during the last two thousand years. As a matter of fact, homelessness is quite an incorrect term for our condition. The Hebrew term *galut* is more exact and more descriptive of the true state of Jewish life during the centuries that followed the destruction of the Temple. *Galut* means banishment. It carries the meaning of exile, but it does not necessarily mean homelessness.

The Jews of Babylonia, after the destruction of the first Temple in 586 B.C.E., were in *galut*. They were a landless people but they certainly were not a homeless people, psychologically speaking. There is a vast psychological difference between landlessness and homelessness. To make a home is quite different from owning a house. The two may be related; they may enhance one another. But having a house of one's own is not a necessary element in the making of a home.

What is the difference between a home and a house? A house is a physical structure—four walls, a floor, a ceiling, doors and windows. A home is basically a psychological structure—a complex of human relationships, associations and activities, of thoughts exchanged and emotions shared, of struggles and conflicts that come and go, of memories and yearnings that persist. "Home" carries with it the meaning of intimacy and familiarity. It signifies relationships that are assumed and consummated. It represents a realm of discourse which the stranger may not fully understand but which requires no articulation for the member of the family. It is the stable ground whose foundations are deeply anchored. It is the secure corner in a world of shifting adjustments.

Jews have been a landless people for nearly two thousand years. But their homelessness dates back only about two hundred years.

From unpublished notes, undated.

The decisive characteristic of eighteenth- and nineteenth-century Judaism is the change in the setting of the historic drama of Israel. Until the modern period, Jewish history was cosmic history. It was part of a divine pattern. With the coming of the modern period, the cosmic history of the Jews is transformed into a social and political history.

In the world of the eighteenth and nineteenth centuries, Jews, because of intellectual integrity or political necessity, begin to reject their distinctiveness, their historic role in the salvation of man. And the chosen people of God almost gleefully abdicate their cosmic function to accept the status of a minority. Their vision of the finger of God guiding them is transposed into the fear of the strong arm of man. As they leave the ghetto for the wider world of the gentiles, they begin their journey into the shrunken one-dimensional world of man. In the framework of man's world, in the economy of earthly power, measured and calculated, they are compelled to accept the historic judgment of the dominant religion—that they are a rejected people.

From unpublished notes, undated.

The well-known phrase, "some of my best friends are Jews," has the interesting though lesser-known counterpart among Jews: "Some of my best friends are gentiles." Like the former, it is susceptible to a variety of nuances. Nevertheless, each of the two phrases, whatever its verbal variations and whatever it may have in common with the other, represents a different realm of human relationships. "Some of my best friends are Jews" is essentially an act of condescension. It is a movement of the powerful—a momentary gesture of communion towards the powerless. It implies a patronizing inclusiveness, a sense of higher status that reaches down to include those of lower status but retains its own position.

"Some of my best friends are gentiles" is an act of *ascension*. It is a movement of the powerless in the direction of the powerful, a reaching upward and towards them, an attempt at a link with them. Implicit in it is *an attempt to change position*, to move forward, not to return.

The former is an act of power. It is spoken by one who, although he is free to accept or reject, chooses to accept. The latter points to powerlessness. It is spoken by one who, in the psychological situation in which he finds himself, can neither accept nor reject. Accustomed to or expecting rejection, he is grateful when accepted.

The different meanings that Jews and gentiles ascribe to these phrases clearly refer to a relationship beyond the immediate persons involved. They are symptoms of the state and nature of the relationship of Jews and non-Jews in the modern world. The basic fact characterizing this relationship is the aspiration of many Jews to change their position and to move towards the gentile world.

From unpublished notes, undated.

Too many Jews and especially too many young Jews live on the periphery of the Jewish community, even when they live among Jews. The tragic becomes the dominant aspect of their background. For on the periphery their interaction is less with Jeremiah and Judah Maccabee and more with Haman and Hitler or their American imitators and disciples. The dominant note in their sense of community with Jews is that of community of suffering. Hence their fractional definition of Jews and Judaism—Judaism is conceived of as disability. They need a more complete and integrated image of themselves, a sense of context and a moral core. Their roots must be deepened and their horizon of Jewish experience extended so that they may perceive its meaning beyond suffering. They must come to know Jewish poets and prophets and leaders of our people as well as the common folk who are alive in law and legend, in symbols and folkways, in home and synagogue, in the whole pattern of Jewish life and thought. And having shared in their spirit, having rooted themselves in their faith, they will bring a passion for justice, love of freedom, devotion to learning— the permanent values of the legacy of Israel—to the American campus.

It is a tragic fact of our existence as Jews that a great religion, the prophetic faith and culture of our people, the cornerstone of morality and religion in the western world, has been reduced in Jewish schools (and often also in synagogues) to a technique of minority adjustment, an antidote to an inferiority complex!

Judaism is capable of giving us more than we have demanded of it. It can give us the ideals and commitments, the resources of faith and thought and insight that we must have to live intelligently and hopefully.

A Jewish education that attempts to address itself to this fateful and difficult enterprise will have to see us and our children as persons—as human-beings-born-Jews—whose problems and concerns cannot be neatly divided into Jewish and human.

It will have to cease being frantically preoccupied with our "survival" as Jews, with Jewish group survival, or with "Jewish consciousness," and it will have to become wisely and deeply concerned with our total lives as Jewish persons.

It will have to help us articulate our innermost questions and needs, and to guide us to the discovery or re-discovery of the ideals and values of Judaism by which Jewish persons can live ethical, creative, and satisfying lives. We shall survive only if we can learn to appropriate these ideals and embody them in our lives, in our homes, and in our institutions.

From unpublished notes, undated.

B asically democracy is a non-force philosophy. It seeks to achieve and guarantee life, liberty, and the pursuit of happiness by means of rational discussion. Not that democracy has already achieved what we ordinarily claim for it. Not that we are innocent of lynching Negroes, of discriminating against Jews, of underpaying workers, and of promoting dissension. We have done all these—we have fallen short of our claims. But we have the virtue of hypocrisy. For it indicates our sense of shame at our present acts or status or mode of thinking, and proclaims that we are what we should be.

We practice inequality but, ashamed to admit it, we insist on our belief in the democratic ideal of equality. Well, hypocrisy indicates a goal other than the immediate act. The recognition of the goal is a moral affirmation in certain principles which human beings because of circumstance, frailty, or corruption are unable to practice at a given time. But insofar as they recognize the immorality of their acts, they do pay homage to virtue and set it up as a goal to be achieved. A sense of shame is morally of great significance. It is an act of conscience.

From unpublished notes, undated.

I came from far away to be here this morning. Yet now, as I stand before you, I feel and am like a stutterer in search of a word most easily articulated, groping for some phrase or image that would capture the meaning of this hour for the friends and disciples of Kurt Lewin. But the heart insists on speaking, although the tongue stumbles, insists on vocalizing, however inadequately, our deep sorrow, and indeed, our thanksgiving that he shared his days and years with us and made his life inextricably linked with ours—his thought part of our thought.

Kurt Lewin was my teacher and friend, and I speak as a humble disciple. I first met him about thirteen years ago at Cornell. Shortly after our meeting I asked him to lead a seminar for the Hillel Foundation on Jewish student adjustment, a subject in which he continued to be interested to the last day of his life. He was then but a stranger in the United

States; he could hardly make himself understood. But he understood the students and they understood him, for he understood so well their problems and predicaments as human-beings-born-Jews. Since then I watched him in the classroom and out of it; at seminars; in his home at Cornell, Berkeley, and Iowa; at public lectures; and in unforgettable face-to-face discussions which lasted, over a cup of tea, until two or three in the morning. And every time I saw him I felt like reciting the traditional benediction of orthodox Jews in the presence of the great: "Blessed art Thou, O Lord our God, who givest of Thy wisdom to mortal man."

The essence of Kurt Lewin's wisdom lay in his profoundly human qualities of sympathy and love for persons, for the suffering and the alienated. He listened to everyone and learned from everyone—a chance conversation in a restaurant, the notions of a student, the criticisms of the learned. He listened to all, for he was a humble and modest person. One would never know from talking to him that he was a world-renowned scientist. He was as eager to learn as to teach—eager to learn that he might teach.

Thus through insight and understanding, through love and sympathy for people, mantled in the humility and contagion of his personality, he crossed the barriers of geography and language into the hearts and minds of men and women. And they became his friends and disciples. They loved him and marveled at him—at his greatness and his simplicity, his playfulness and humor, his childlike innocence and his profound insights, his daring, his dynamism.

Kurt Lewin was a scientist. But there was a breath-taking sweep about his scientific effort, about his vision of the possibility of one conceptual framework for all the social sciences. And there was something that I might call religious about Lewin the scientist. Religious, in his selfless dedication to the truth as he saw it and as he found it—religious, above all, in the goal of his scientific efforts, in his ethical ends, in the social direction which he gave to his work.

The social character of his effort is best indicated in the phrase that he used and made popular in recent years. He liked to speak of his scientific work at MIT and CCI (Commission on Community Interrelations of the American Jewish Congress) as "action research." It is a good phrase. It describes, I think, both his method and his goal. For Kurt Lewin was not an ivory-towered social scientist—a statistical analyst of human traits, a maker of theories. He wished to fuse the thought and the act, to transmute theory into a mechanism for social living, and out of social interaction to derive concepts and techniques relevant to human need and suffering. He tried the difficult task, perhaps the impossible. But he knew the truth of the rabbinic saying, *La alecha ham'lacha ligmor, v'en atah ben horin l'hitpater mimena*—"It is not for you to complete the task, neither are you free to desist from it." That was the compulsion, manifested in his life and work, which made him give himself selflessly and unsparingly to the service of his fellowmen.

It was that compulsion, intensified by personal sorrow, which drove him to apply his scientific method to the community of Jews whose fate he shared. He had long been interested in the problems of Jewish maladjustment as an aspect of minority life. The tragedy of Jews in Germany, his own experience of exile (his mother died in a concentration camp) deepened his interest in the fate of Jews in our time. He became teacher and guide of young Jews. They became his special concern, and in recent years he spent much time on the problems of Jewish education and the fate of the Jewish child in a world of fear and discrimination. He articulated the fears of Jews and their timidities. He analyzed their source and he gave Jews a mirror-image of themselves. But he was more than analyst. He translated his findings into an interpretation of the function of Jewish education. Beyond its values in the transmission of the Jewish heritage, he urged that Jewish education must help Jews affirm themselves, giving them security and status through self-affirmation.

And he was convinced, especially in more recent years, that the path to self-affirmation must ultimately lead to Zionism. For Zionism, to him, was more than the building of a state, more than a refuge for suffering Jews. The value of Zionism, its ultimate human significance, was in its effect upon the Jewish personality. Its redemptive power would heal body and spirit alike. It would emancipate Jews from fear, from self-hatred. And Palestine became to him, in a real sense, the great laboratory where his experimental findings at Iowa, MIT, and CCI would be confirmed; the effect of social atmosphere on human personality would be magnificently demonstrated.

And now he is no longer with us—no longer to share in the projects he founded and directed, no longer to execute his plans. But his disciples are here, and he shares, beyond the immortality which is hidden from the sight of man, that immortality which is assured to the wise and their disciples. For his thoughts will fructify the search for knowledge and freedom, and his life, his self-dedication, his kindness, his simplicity and modesty, will continue to inspire his disciples and their disciples to emulate him and to be guided by his example.

As I say farewell to my dear friend, *Shalom* (Peace!)—the greeting that he liked so much—I pray there may be a measure of consolation to the friends and relatives of Kurt Lewin. May God grant peace and strength to his wife and children who shared his life and shared his faith, who built his home and surrounded him with that joy and happiness which his enthusiasm and cheerfulness made manifest.

The memory of the righteous is a blessing. The Lord

giveth; the Lord taketh away; blessed be the name of the Lord.

*Eulogy delivered at funeral
of Dr. Kurt Lewin,
Cambridge, Massachusetts,
February 14, 1947.*

POSTSCRIPT: REMARKS AT A
HILLEL ORIENTATION

The other day my wife was rummaging through some of my papers—I call them the "Pekarsky fragments"—and she came across a sheet of paper on which I had scribbled some notes for a talk I delivered at Cornell University in November, 1933, just about five months after I had been ordained a rabbi. The subject of my talk was "A Rabbi Looks Back."

Believe me, in November, 1933, I had very little to look back upon as a rabbi. And I smiled at my youthful pretense in presuming to suggest that I was a man of vast experience and could bring a new revelation to the students at Cornell University.

As my wife was going to throw my touch of greatness into the wastepaper basket, I thought I should be no less fair to myself than I try to be to others, and I took a look at what I had said. It was not quite as bad as I had thought. I had emphasized that a rabbi who looks back, should look back upon the time when he was *not* a rabbi—when he was a student, sitting as you do now, listening to those who preach at him. I suggested that whenever he stood before a class or his congregation, he should remember when he had been a member of the class and try to sense that affinity of spirit and concern by recalling the questions he used to ask, his own rebellion, his own heresies and doubts. They might protect him, I thought, from the corrupting and corroding sin of talking to himself or of addressing the world, but not the persons directly in front of him.

I have tried to the best of my ability to live that way—to remember my questions, my irritations when I listened to preachers and professors who thought they were (or acted as if they were) the voice of God, experience, or truth, but whose performance did not seem to justify the impression they were trying to make. In the same way, in my contact with students, I have tried to recall the questions students ask, their concerns, their predicaments upon coming to a university.

From unpublished notes,
prepared for address to
students, B'nai B'rith Hillel
Foundation at the University
of Chicago, October 7, 1957.